STUNNING JEWELRY

❋ made easy

LEISURE ARTS, INC.
Little Rock, Arkansas

EDITORIAL STAFF

Editor-in-Chief: Susan White Sullivan
Craft Publications Director: Cheryl Johnson
Special Projects Director: Susan Frantz Wiles
Senior Prepress Director: Mark Hawkins
Art Publications Director: Rhonda Shelby
Technical Editor: Mary Sullivan Hutcheson
Technical Writer: Lisa Lancaster
Editorial Writer: Susan McManus Johnson
Art Category Manager: Lora Puls
Lead Graphic Artist: Kara Darling
Graphic Artist: Jacob Casleton
Imaging Technician: Stephanie Johnson
Prepress Technician: Janie Marie Wright
Photography Manager: Katherine Laughlin
Contributing Photographers: Mark Mathews
     and Ken West
Contributing Photo Stylists: Sondra Daniel
     and Christy Myers
Publishing Systems Administrator: Becky Riddle
Mac Information Technology Specialist: Robert Young

BUSINESS STAFF

President and Chief Executive Officer: Rick Barton
Vice President of Sales: Mike Behar
Director of Finance and Administration:
     Laticia Mull Dittrich
National Sales Director: Martha Adams
Creative Services: Chaska Lucas
Information Technology Director: Hermine Linz
Controller: Francis Caple
Vice President, Operations: Jim Dittrich
Retail Customer Service Manager: Stan Raynor
Print Production Manager: Fred F. Pruss

Library of Congress Control Number: 2011933649
ISBN-13: 978-1-60900-307-4

TABLE OF CONTENTS

Learn a different jewelry-making technique with each of these 20 exciting designs! Half the projects are beginner-friendly, while the rest kick up the intensity, giving you even more ways to amaze yourself. Discover how to knot leather and fashion a custom toggle clasp. Create bead dangles by the dozens. Learn classic bead weaving patterns, such as Peyote Stitch and Square Stitch. And cast resin into a large, lightweight pendant. The photos take you right into the details, while clear instructions guide you to make sparkling necklaces, pendants, and bracelets. Whether elegantly simple or bold with texture, your original jewelry will thrill the designer in you!

DESIGNER SVETLANA KUNINA

…says her whole life has been connected to the arts, with generous inspiration from many cultures.

"I feel blessed to have grown up in Russia, where there is a huge emphasis on arts and crafts," Svetlana explains. "Starting in kindergarten, we made holiday gifts for our parents and loved ones. We learned all kinds of crafts in school, and I even designed and made my own clothes on my mother's sewing machine.

"I've been lucky to travel to many European countries such as Spain, Germany, and Switzerland. I've also been fortunate to travel around the United States, where I now live. Learning about different cultures has had a big impact in shaping my creative vision.

"Several years ago, I saw a beautiful hand-woven bracelet; it gripped my heart. I took a class in bead weaving and learned Peyote Stitch. After that first bracelet, the ideas started flowing for original designs. I began selling patterns and kits and created a Web site for this purpose at www.BeadKnots.com. When I started selling my work at art shows and boutiques, I created another Web site at www.NecessaryJewelry.com featuring my jewelry for sale.

"I discovered that I really like teaching the skill of beading. For me, there is nothing better than to hear a happy 'Oh, I get it now!' I enjoy inspiring my students to explore different options and colors. There are times when each student leaves the class with a distinctive piece of jewelry, even though we all started with the same pattern.

"Like my classes, this book takes different techniques and shows how they can be merged together to create stunning jewelry pieces. There are easy and advanced techniques, so as you learn the basics you can continue to explore more.

"When I'm not working, I spend time with my bulldog Feodor (named after the Russian writer Feodor Dostoevski). I listen to music, dance the tango, grow vegetables in my garden, and volunteer for community projects. I love getting together with my friends to create art.

"Jewelry-making brings so much joy and peace that I want to continue inspiring people to do it. So, stay busy creating! Enjoy and have fun!"

DELICATE NECKLACE WITH LOCKET

This airy necklace is easy to create when you lay out the beads on a bead board. A removable pendant is a breeze to make with a bail that opens and closes.

Skill Level: Easy

Locket Size: 1" x 1½"

Supplies You'll Need
Materials:
- 4 18mm turquoise ceramic ring beads
- 10 4mm copper crystal bicone beads
- 10 4mm light blue crystal bicone beads
- 4 8mm light topaz crystal round beads
- 4 8mm light aqua crystal round beads
- 2 10mm antique silver corrugated rondelle beads
- 2 8mm silver rondelle spacer beads
- 8 silver metal spacer beads
- 1" x 1½" antique silver oval locket pendant
- Beadalon® silver interchangeable enhancer bail
- 1.2mm silver crimp tubes
- Silver lobster clasp with crimp ends
- 19 strand silver nylon-coated stringing wire .018" dia.

Tools:
- Chain-nose pliers
- Flat-nose pliers
- Wire cutters
- Crimping pliers
- Bead board

Refer to General Instructions (pages 82-89) before beginning.

Continued on page 8.

Delicate Necklace with Locket continued from page 6.

Instructions

1. Position the pendant on the bead board at the "0" mark. Place the following bead sequences, moving to the right from the center and allowing about 1" of wire between each sequence:

Sequence #1:
- crimp tube (placed 1" to the right of center)
- copper crystal bicone bead
- antique silver corrugated rondelle bead
- copper crystal bicone bead
- crimp tube

Sequence #2:
- crimp tube
- light blue crystal bicone bead
- light topaz crystal round bead
- silver metal spacer bead
- ceramic ring bead with light blue crystal bicone bead in center
- silver metal spacer bead
- light topaz crystal round bead
- light blue crystal bicone bead
- crimp tube

Sequence #3:
- crimp tube
- copper crystal bicone bead
- light aqua crystal round bead
- silver metal spacer bead
- ceramic ring bead with copper crystal bicone bead in center
- silver metal spacer bead
- light aqua crystal round bead
- copper crystal bicone bead
- crimp tube

Sequence #4:
- crimp tube
- light blue crystal bicone bead
- silver rondelle spacer bead
- light blue crystal bicone bead
- crimp tube

2. Repeat Sequences 1-4 on the left side of the bead board.

3. Cut about 20" of stringing wire.

4. Slide on the crimp tube from Sequence 1. Slide the crimp tube to about 1" to the right of the center; crimp. Slide on all the Sequence 1 beads, making sure they fit snugly together; crimp the final crimp tube to close the sequence.

5. Attach Sequences 2, 3 and 4, one by one, on the right side. Refer to **Photo 1** when stringing the ceramic ring beads with the crystal bicone beads in the center.

6. Repeat Steps 4-5 for the left side of the necklace.

7. To attach the clasp, place a crimp end into the first chamber of the crimping pliers **(Photo 2)**. Insert the wire all the way into the crimp end, until you see the wire coming out the other side. Slowly slide the wire back to hide the end inside the crimp end. Firmly press to secure the crimp end **(Photo 3)**. Repeat with the remaining crimp end on the other side of the necklace.

8. Gently open the small ring on the bail, slide the pendant onto the ring, and close the ring. Open the bail and hang it in the middle of the necklace.

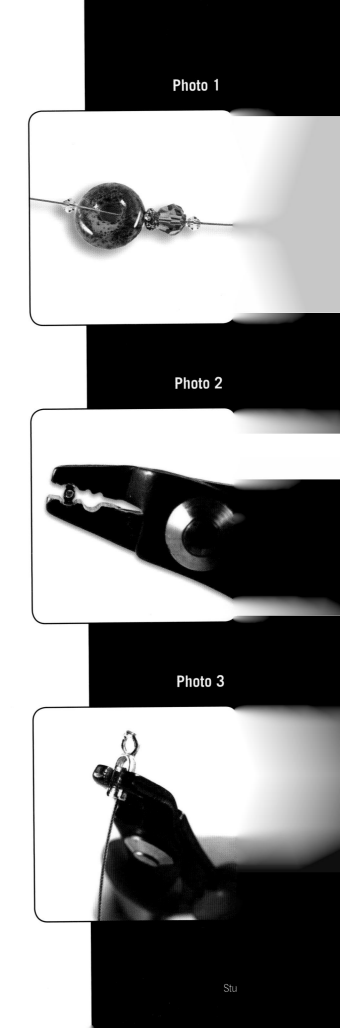

Photo 1

Photo 2

Photo 3

Stu

MOSAIC PENDANT NECKLACE

A simple mosaic design is easy to create on a basic metal washer from the hardware store.

Skill Level: Easy

Pendant Size: 1¹/₂" diameter

Supplies You'll Need
Materials:
- 1¹/₂" dia. metal washer (from the hardware store)
- Assorted seed beads (size 11/0)
- Assorted 4mm and 6mm faceted glass beads
- Assorted glass beads in various sizes, shapes, and colors to use as accents
- Black 2mm round leather cord
- 2 silver crimp tubes with loop ends
- Silver lobster clasp with attached jump ring
- 4mm silver jump ring

Tools:
- Chain-nose pliers
- Flat-nose pliers
- Tweezers
- Bead mat
- E-6000® Industrial Strength Adhesive
- Rubbing alcohol wipes
- Sanding block (220 grit/very fine)

Refer to General Instructions (pages 82-89) before beginning.

Continued on page 12.

Mosaic Pendant continued from page 10.

Instructions

1. Polish both sides of the washer with the sanding block, using gentle strokes, all going in one direction. Wipe away the dust with alcohol wipes and let dry. Be careful to not get fingerprints on the washer.

2. Place the beads on the bead mat. Working within a $1\frac{1}{2}$" dia. circle, play with different arrangements to create the one you like. Try positioning the larger beads first, concentrating on one section of the circle, say the bottom half. Then fill the smaller areas with seed beads, sprinkling the beads as if you were decorating cookies. Once you are happy with your arrangement, set it aside.

3. Place the washer on a clean, flat work surface. Use a scrap piece of cardboard to spread a thin layer of adhesive on the washer.

4. Use tweezers to pick up the larger beads one by one and place them on the washer, following your arrangement. Press the beads gently into the adhesive. Don't press too hard; this can cause the adhesive to ooze from under the bead.

5. Sprinkle the smaller beads around the large ones, so that the entire washer surface is covered. Use tweezers to tweak the arrangement. If you get glue on the tweezers, wipe off with the alcohol wipes.

6. Let dry overnight.

7. Place the completed pendant wrong side up. Cut a piece of leather cord about $3\frac{1}{2}$" longer than the desired finished necklace length. Fold the cord in half, creating a loop in the middle. Insert the loop from front to back into the washer hole. Pull the ends through the loop and tighten *(Fig. 1)*.

8. Finish the leather cord ends (page 89) and attach the clasp. Attach a jump ring to the remaining cord end.

Fig. 1

Red, Black, & Pearl Bracelet

Use a bead board to design a custom-sized bracelet. I've listed the number of beads I used for a 7" long bracelet (not including the clasp).

Skill Level: Easy

Supplies You'll Need
Materials:
- 18mm flat disc red ceramic bead
- 2 13mm x 15mm topaz glass teardrop pearls
- 2 8mm topaz glass round pearls
- 2 4mm topaz glass round pearls
- 4 8mm x 10mm black/gold rectangular windowpane beads
- 2 6mm faceted black/gold beads
- 4 8mm silver rondelle spacer beads
- 4 5mm 3-sided silver spacer beads
- 2 5mm silver round eye spacer beads
- Silver toggle clasp with attached jump ring
- 2 6mm silver solid rings
- Silver crimp tubes
- 49 strand silver nylon-coated stringing wire .018" dia.

Tools:
- Chain-nose pliers
- Flat-nose pliers
- Wire cutters
- Crimping pliers
- Bead board
- 2 bead stoppers

Refer to General Instructions (pages 82-89) before beginning.

Continued on page 14.

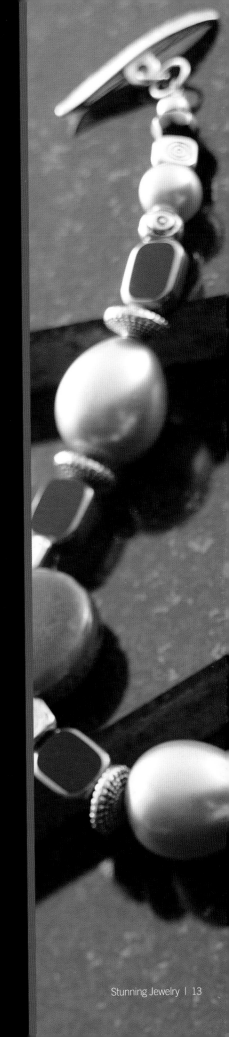

Red, Black, & Pearl Bracelet continued from page 13.

Instructions

1. To determine the size of your bracelet:
   Measure your wrist slightly below the
   wrist bone. Add 1"-1¹/₂" for wearing ease,
   depending on how loose you like wearing
   bracelets. Measure the size of the closed clasp
   and subtract that.
   *For example: My wrist is 6". I like my bracelets
   a bit loose, and my closed clasp is 1".
   Here's the math:*
   6" + 1¹/₂" = 7¹/₂"
   (wrist size + wearing ease)
   7¹/₂" – 1" = 6¹/₂" is my bracelet size
   (determined measurement – clasp size)

2. Position the beads on the bead board, starting
   in the center, next to the "0" mark with the
   red ceramic bead. Place the following bead
   sequence, working in either direction from the
   center:
   - 3-sided silver spacer bead
   - black/gold rectangular windowpane bead
   - silver rondelle spacer bead
   - topaz teardrop pearl
   - silver rondelle spacer bead
   - black/gold rectangular windowpane bead
   - silver round eye spacer bead
   - 8mm topaz round pearl
   - 3-sided silver spacer bead
   - faceted black/gold bead
   - 4mm topaz round pearl

3. Repeat the sequence on the other side.

4. Check the bead layout measurement to be
   sure it is the finished size you calculated
   earlier. Now is the time to add or subtract
   beads to customize the bracelet size.

5. Using the wire cutters, cut a length of stringing
   wire the bracelet size plus 2". Place a bead
   stopper near one wire end to prevent the
   beads from sliding off.

6. String on the beads one by one from the bead
   board. Place a bead stopper on the end.

7. Remove one bead stopper and finish one wire
   end of the bracelet with a solid ring and crimp
   tube (page 89).

8. Slide the beads against the finished end and
   repeat Step 7.

9. Attach the clasp.

FUCHSIA PENDANT NECKLACE

Suspend a beautiful glass bead from an easy-to-make jump ring chain.

Skill Level: Easy

Pendant Size: 1" diameter

Supplies You'll Need
Materials:
- 10 4mm silver jump rings
- 6mm x 7.5mm silver oval jump ring
- 2" silver head pin with ball head
- 6mm fuchsia-colored faceted glass bead
- 25mm silver textured solid ring
- 2 silver crimp tubes with loop ends
- Black 2mm round leather cord
- Silver lobster clasp with attached jump ring

Tools:
- Chain-nose pliers
- Flat-nose pliers
- Round-nose pliers
- Wire cutters

Refer to General Instructions (pages 82-89) before beginning.

Continued on page 18.

Fuchsia Pendant Necklace continued from page 16.

Instructions

1. Open a 4mm jump ring, slide on 2 jump rings, and close the jump ring. You have just made a chain of 3 jump rings *(Fig. 1)*.

2. Repeat Step 1 to make 3 groups of 3 jump rings. Join the groups together to make a chain that is 9 jump rings long.

3. Open another jump ring and connect it to the middle jump ring (the 5th one from the end) of the chain; do not close the jump ring yet. Slide on the oval jump ring, and close the jump ring. The ends of the chain stay loose.

4. Slide the bead onto the head pin. Trim the head pin ¹/₂" above the bead. Using the round-nose pliers, make a loop.

5. Wrap the chain around the textured ring. Open the loop on the head pin, slide the loose ends of the chain onto the head pin and close the loop.

6. Cut the desired length of leather cord. Thread the leather cord through the oval jump ring. Finish the leather cord ends (page 89) and attach the clasp.

Fig. 1

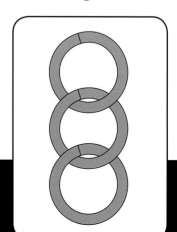

LEATHER BAND WITH FLOWERS

Combine a leather band, suede flower shapes, and sparkly crystals for a cool bracelet.

Skill Level: Easy

Supplies You'll Need
Materials:
- Black Realeather® Jewelry slide bracelet (³/₄" x 9")
- 7 Realeather® Jewelry assorted suede flowers (lavender, purple, yellow, and orange)
- 7 8mm silver rondelle spacer beads
- 4 4mm rose AB crystal bicone beads
- 3 4mm copper crystal bicone beads
- 7 2" silver head pins with ball heads

Tools:
- Chain-nose pliers
- Flat-nose pliers
- Wire cutters
- Hole punch for leather
- Light-colored fine-point marker

Refer to General Instructions (pages 82-89) before beginning.

Continued on page 20.

Leather Band with Flowers continued from page 19.

Photo 1

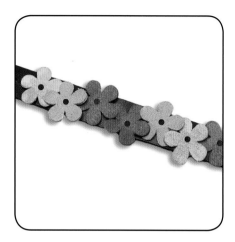

Instructions

1. Lay the bracelet right side up on the cutting mat. Arrange the flowers, slightly overlapping each other in a wave pattern **(Photo 1)**.

2. Use the light-colored marker to mark each flower center on the bracelet. Remove the flowers and set aside.

3. Punch the marked holes with the smallest diameter punch on the leather hole punch. Then add another hole about $1/8$" away from the first hole **(Photo 2)**.

4. Slide the following sequence on a head pin:
- crystal bicone bead
- silver rondelle spacer bead
- suede flower.

5. Put the head pin through a punched hole on the bracelet. Using chain-nose pliers, bend the pin at a 90° angle. Move the pliers about $1/8$" and bend another 90° angle toward the bracelet. Insert this bent end into the nearby hole of the bracelet.

6. Hold the head pin with the chain-nose pliers between the leather band and the flower. Use the flat-nose pliers to wrap the end around the head pin. Make 3-4 wraps to secure the head pin **(Fig. 1)**. Cut off the excess wire.

7. Repeat Steps 4-6 to attach each flower to the bracelet.

Photo 2

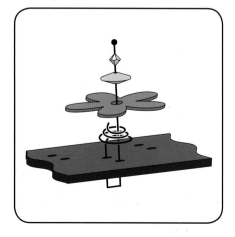

Fig. 1

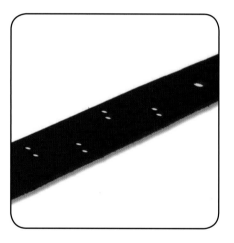

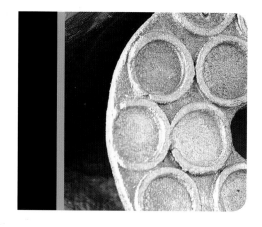

SCULPTED PENDANT NECKLACE

Create your own resin pendant by making a reusable flexible rubber mold. Add the pendant to a necklace that has multiple bead sequences.

Skill Level: Easy

Pendant Size: 1³/₄" diameter

Supplies You'll Need
Materials:
- Amazing Mold Putty kit
- Amazing Casting Resin kit
- 1³/₄" dia. metal washer with a ⁵/₁₆" hole (from the hardware store)
- 16-18 10mm jump rings (2mm thick)
- Jacquard Lumiere® true gold (#550) light body metallic acrylic
- Jacquard Pearl Ex silver (#663) powdered pigment
- 4 11mm x 15mm black/silver windowpane hex beads
- 12 6mm black/gold faceted beads
- 2 8mm black/gold faceted beads
- 8 4mm topaz round glass pearls
- 2 8mm topaz round glass pearls
- 4 4mm silver metal round beads
- 1.2mm silver crimp tubes
- Silver lobster clasp with attached jump ring
- 6mm x 7.5mm silver oval jump ring
- 2 6mm silver solid rings
- 19 strand silver nylon-coated stringing wire .015" dia.

Tools:
- Chain-nose pliers
- Flat-nose pliers
- Wire cutters
- Crimping pliers
- Assorted files for sanding and smoothing
- Awl
- Bead board
- ¹/₄" and ¹/₈" stencil brushes

Continued on page 24.

Sculpted Pendant Necklace continued from page 22.

Refer to General Instructions (pages 82-89) before beginning.

Instructions
Making a Mold

1. Follow the manufacturer's instructions to make a golf ball size ball of Amazing Putty. Press the metal washer into the putty **(Photo 1)**; remove the washer quickly and carefully to preserve the shape.

2. Place the 10mm jump rings in the mold **(Photo 2)**, place the washer on top and press into the mold again. Remove the washer and jump rings. You need to work as quickly as possible, taking about 1-2 minutes to complete this whole process.

3. Let the mold cure.

Making a Pendant with the Mold

1. Follow the manufacturer's instructions to prepare a small amount of Amazing Casting Resin.

2. Place the mold on a sturdy, flat, covered work surface. Carefully pour the resin into the mold. Do not overfill; pour just enough to reach the top edges of the mold **(Photo 3)**.

3. Let the resin cure.

4. Remove the pendant from the mold. Use the files to rough up the pendant surface and smooth out any imperfections or uneven areas. Make sturdy, firm strokes, moving in one direction only.

5. Punch a hole with the awl, twisting and pushing gently as you go through the pendant.

Photo 1　　　　**Photo 2**　　　　**Photo 3**

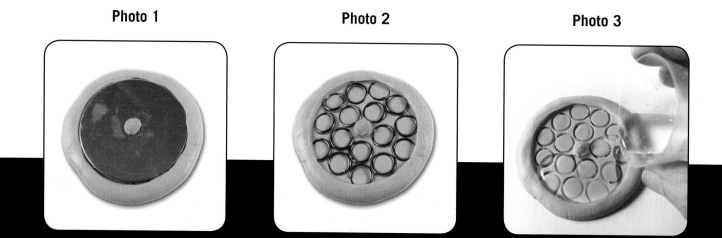

6. Use the $1/4$" stencil brush and light dabbing motions to apply the gold paint. You may need to go over some spots several times to get complete coverage and desired color. While the paint is still wet, apply small amounts of silver powdered pigment; gently press the powder into the paint with the $1/8$" stencil brush. Let dry overnight.

Making the Necklace

1. Position the beads on the bead board, starting in the center, next to the "0" mark. Place the pendant at "0". Place the following bead sequences, moving to the right from the center and allowing about 1" of wire between each sequence:

Sequence #1:
- crimp tube
- 4mm topaz round pearl
- 6mm black/gold faceted bead
- black/silver windowpane hex bead
- 6mm black/gold faceted bead
- 4mm topaz round pearl
- crimp tube

Sequence #2:
- crimp tube
- silver metal round bead
- 8mm black/gold faceted bead
- silver metal round bead
- crimp tube

Sequence #3: Repeat Sequence #1

Sequence #4:
- crimp tube
- 6mm black/gold faceted bead
- 8mm topaz round pearl
- 6mm black/gold faceted bead
- crimp tube

2. Repeat Sequences 1-4 on the left side of the bead board.

3. Cut about 22" of stringing wire.

4. Slide on the first crimp tube from Sequence 1. Slide the crimp tube to about 1" to the right of the center; crimp. Slide on all the Sequence 1 beads, making sure they fit snugly together; crimp the final crimp tube to close the sequence.

5. Attach Sequences 2, 3 and 4, one by one, on the right side.

6. Repeat Steps 4-5 for the left side of the necklace.

7. Finish each end of the necklace with a solid ring, leaving about $1/2$" of exposed wire after the last bead sequences.

8. Attach the clasp with the jump ring.

9. Attach the pendant to the middle of the necklace with the oval jump ring.

WOVEN LEATHER BRACELET

Suede lace comes in a wide range of colors and is quite easy to fashion into a casual bracelet with a bit of bling. The soft suede is easy to knot.

Skill Level: Easy

Supplies You'll Need
Materials:
- On-A-Cord® $^3/_{32}$" aqua Sof-Suede Lace
- On-A-Cord® $^3/_{32}$" cafe Sof-Suede Lace
- 8 3mm x 6mm silver metal spacer beads
- 4 4mm silver round eye beads
- Jolee's jewels™ Crystallized™ Swarovski Elements (bermuda blue square ring pendant)
- Realeather® Jewelry flower bud end caps with attached clasp
- Beadalon® silver interchangeable enhancer bail
- 6mm silver jump ring

Tools:
- Chain-nose pliers
- Flat-nose pliers
- Aleene's® Jewelry & Metal Glue™

Refer to General Instructions (pages 82-89) before beginning.

Continued on page 28.

Woven Leather Bracelet continued from page 26.

Instructions

*Each group of 16 knots is approximately 1¹/₂"
long. To make the bracelet longer, start with a
longer length of each suede lace and increase
the number of knots in each group.*

1. Cut a 1 yard length of each suede lace. Lay
the cafe lace on the work surface. Tie the
aqua lace around the middle of the cafe lace
(Fig. 1). Tie the cafe lace around the aqua
lace *(Photo 1)*.

2. Using 1 cafe lace and 1 aqua lace, tie an
overhand knot, just like the one you use when
beginning to tie your shoes. Using the other
cafe lace and the other aqua lace, tie another
overhand knot *(Photo 2)*. Notice how each
knot sits on top of the previous knot. Continue
tying knots, alternating laces, for a total of 16
knots.

3. Slide a silver spacer bead on each cord and
continue tying 16 knots *(Photo 3)*.

4. Slide a silver round bead on each cord and
continue tying 16 knots.

5. Repeat Step 3.

7. Tie 16 more knots. Trim the excess suede.

8. Place a dab of glue in an end cap and insert
one bracelet end, twisting the bracelet until
the suede ends are snug and all the way in
the cap. Repeat with the remaining end cap
on the opposite end. Let dry overnight.

9. Attach the jump ring to the ring on the bail; do
not close the ring. Slide the open ring through
the hole on a round eye bead; close the jump
ring *(Photo 4)*. Open the bail and slide on the
crystal square pendant.

Fig. 1	**Photo 1**	**Photo 2**	**Photo 3**	**Photo 4**

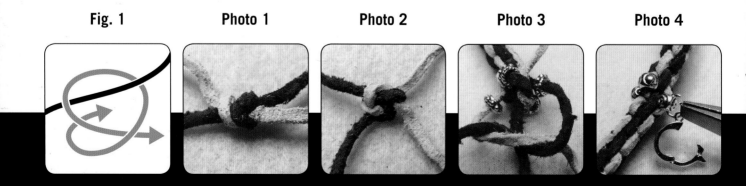

TOWER PENDANT NECKLACE

Peyote Stitch is an easy, yet intricate looking, type of beadwork. A small amount of this beadwork can be joined into a miniature tube to create an interesting "bead."

Skill Level: Easy

Pendant Size: 1³/₄" long

Supplies You'll Need
Materials:
- Size 11/0 Japanese cylinder beads in matte gold
- 12mm black flat disc bead
- 7mm x 5mm rectangular garnet gemstone
- 6mm wine faceted glass round bead
- 6mm golden olive freshwater pearl
- 4mm golden olive freshwater pearl
- 4mm gold faceted glass round bead
- 4mm silver round bead
- 2 6mm silver bead caps
- 2" silver head pin with ball head
- Silver lobster clasp with attached jump ring
- 2 silver crimp tubes with loop ends
- Salmon 2mm leather cord
- Beadalon® Wild Fire™ black beading thread .006" dia.

Tools:
- Chain-nose pliers
- Flat-nose pliers
- Round-nose pliers
- Wire cutters
- Size 10 beading needle

Refer to General Instructions (pages 82-89) and Beadwork Techniques (pages 90-93) before beginning.

Continued on page 30.

Tower Pendant Necklace continued from page 29.

Instructions

Making a Woven Bead Tube

1. Thread the needle with a comfortable length of beading thread and attach an anchor bead. Pick up 6 cylinder beads to begin working Peyote Stitch (pages 92-93). Work Peyote Stitch until you have 12 rows *(Photo 1)*.

2. Fold the woven bead piece into a tube and connect the end beads in a zigzag pattern *(Fig. 1)*.

3. Remove the anchor bead and tie 3 half hitch knots with the working thread and the beginning tail. Secure and end the threads.

Photo 1

Fig. 1

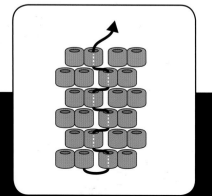

Making the Necklace

1. To make the pendant, slide the following bead sequence on the head pin:
  - 6mm golden olive freshwater pearl
  - gold faceted round bead
  - garnet gemstone
  - 4mm golden olive freshwater pearl
  - black flat disc bead
  - silver round bead
  - woven bead tube *(When adding the woven bead tube, find the center and gently push and twist the head pin between the beads.)*
  - silver bead cap
  - wine faceted glass round bead
  - silver bead cap

2. Leave about ½" and trim the excess wire from the head pin. Using the round-nose pliers, make a loop on the head pin.

3. Cut the desired length of leather cord and slide on the pendant. Finish the leather cord ends (page 89) and attach the clasp.

LEATHER & CHAIN LEAF PENDANT NECKLACE

Pre-cut suede shapes and a metal focal piece combine with beads, braided leather, and a cable chain for a great-looking necklace.

Skill Level: Easy

Pendant Size: 1¹/₂" x 1"

Supplies You'll Need
Materials:
- 2 7mm x 9mm antique silver corrugated rondelle beads
- 2 5mm 3-sided silver spacer beads
- 2 5mm copper round eye spacer beads
- 2 14mm copper flat diamond beads
- Realeather® Jewelry silver floral vine double focal piece
- Realeather® Jewelry assorted leaf and oval suede shapes
- Realeather® Jewelry round leafy end caps with attached clasp and extension chains
- Realeather® CraftLace™ 3mm cognac round braided leather
- 2 4mm silver solid rings
- 6mm silver jump rings
- 2mm silver crimp tubes
- Silver 3.4mm elongated cable chain
- 19 strand silver nylon-coated stringing wire .015" dia.

Tools:
- Chain-nose pliers
- Flat-nose pliers
- Wire cutters
- Flat screwdriver
- Aleene's® Jewelry & Metal Glue™

Refer to General Instructions (pages 82-89) before beginning.

Continued on page 34.

Leather & Chain Leaf Pendant Necklace continued from page 32.

Instructions

The lobster clasp hooks to a solid ring on the side of the pendant. Having a clasp near the front makes the necklace easier to open and close.

1. Use the screwdriver to remove the screws from the focal piece. Stack a suede leaf and a suede oval; place the focal piece on top and reattach the screws to complete the pendant. The leaf is the wrong side of the pendant.

2. Cut about 6" of wire. Fold in half and place the loop around one of the screws on the wrong side of the pendant. Holding the wire ends together, slide a crimp tube on the wires, getting as close as possible to the screw. Press with the chain-nose pliers to flatten and secure the crimp **(Photo 1)**.

3. String the following bead sequence on the wires:
- 3-sided silver spacer bead
- copper flat diamond bead
- antique silver corrugated rondelle bead
- copper round eye spacer bead
- crimp tube

Pass both wire ends through a solid ring and then back through the crimp tube **(Photo 2)**. Tighten the wires to make the loop small and almost hidden inside the copper round bead. Press with the chain-nose pliers to flatten and secure the crimp.

4. Repeat Steps 2 and 3 on the other side of the pendant.

5. Remove the extension chains from the end caps; set the lobster clasp aside for now. Cut the desired length of the braided leather. Place a dab of glue in an end cap and insert one braided leather end, twisting the leather until it is snug and all the way in the cap. Repeat with the remaining end cap on the opposite end. Let dry overnight.

6. For the chain portion of the necklace, cut a length of cable chain a bit longer than the braided leather. Use a jump ring to attach the clasp and one end of the cable chain to one end cap.

7. Use a jump ring to attach one end of the pendant to the cable chain and the remaining end cap.

Photo 1

Photo 2

FUSED GLASS PENDANT NECKLACE

You can make a fused glass pendant in your own home with a small kiln that fits in the microwave. The sliding knot closure allows the necklace to be adjusted.

Skill Level: Easy

Pendant Size: 1" diameter

Supplies You'll Need
Materials:
Fuseworks™ also makes a Beginner's Fusing Kit that includes the kiln, kiln paper, and hot mitts.
- Diamond Tech Fuseworks™ microwave kiln
- Diamond Tech Fuseworks™ kiln paper
- Diamond Tech Fuseworks™ ebony and ivory fusible shapes
- Diamond Tech Fuseworks™ Fuse Art flower decals
- Diamond Tech Fuseworks™ silver round pendant plate
- Diamond Tech Fuseworks™ hot mitts
- On-A-Cord® 3/32" light blue Sof-Suede Lace
- 1 yard 1/8" tan deerskin lace
- 4 8mm silver rondelle spacer beads

Tools:
- Tweezers
- Microwave oven (800-1200 watts)
- White vinegar
- Brown paper towels
- Brick or large ceramic tile to serve as a fireproof surface
- Safety glasses
- Aleene's® Jewelry & Metal Glue™

Continued on page 36.

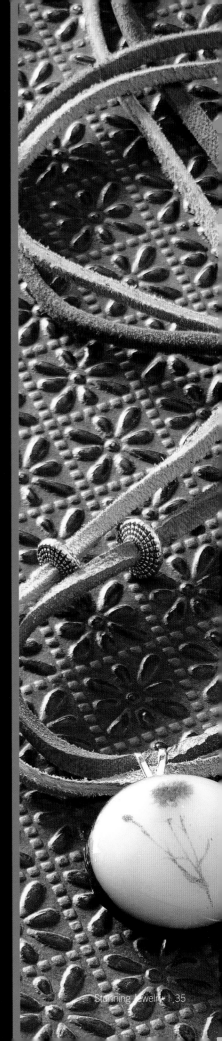

Fused Glass Pendant Necklace continued from page 35.

Instructions

Preparing the Microwave and Kiln for Fusing

1. Read the kiln instruction manual to make sure you properly prepare the kiln for firing. Wear safety glasses when working with the kiln and glass. Follow all safety instructions.

2. It's best to have the microwave oven at waist level, on a counter or table. Place the brick or large ceramic tile to the right of the microwave, serving as a landing spot for the kiln while it is hot. The landing spot has to be fireproof and away from any objects that may catch fire.

3. While the kiln is cold, practice opening the microwave door, taking the kiln out while wearing the hot mitts, and placing it on the fireproof surface. Lift the kiln cover for a few seconds to take a look inside. Now reverse the process, placing the kiln back in the microwave. Do this several times so you'll feel comfortable handling the kiln. You'll need to move the kiln quickly during the process of fusing and it will be very hot.

Fusing the Pendant

1. Cut a 2" square of the kiln paper and place it, smooth side up, in the middle of the kiln base (the bottom part of the kiln). Leave the cover off at this point.

2. In a small bowl, mix 1 part vinegar with 2 parts lukewarm water. Clean one ivory fusible shape and one ebony fusible shape thoroughly with this mixture. Be sure to remove all dust and any fingerprints or spots. Handle the shapes with care to prevent cutting yourself as the glass may have sharp edges. Wipe the shapes dry with brown paper towels, making sure there are no lint pieces and that the glass is completely dry.

3. Using tweezers, center the ebony shape on the kiln paper; place the ivory shape precisely on top of the ebony shape *(Photo 1)*. Place the kiln base in the microwave, making sure the glass shapes don't move. Replace the cover very carefully.

Continued on page 38.

Photo 1

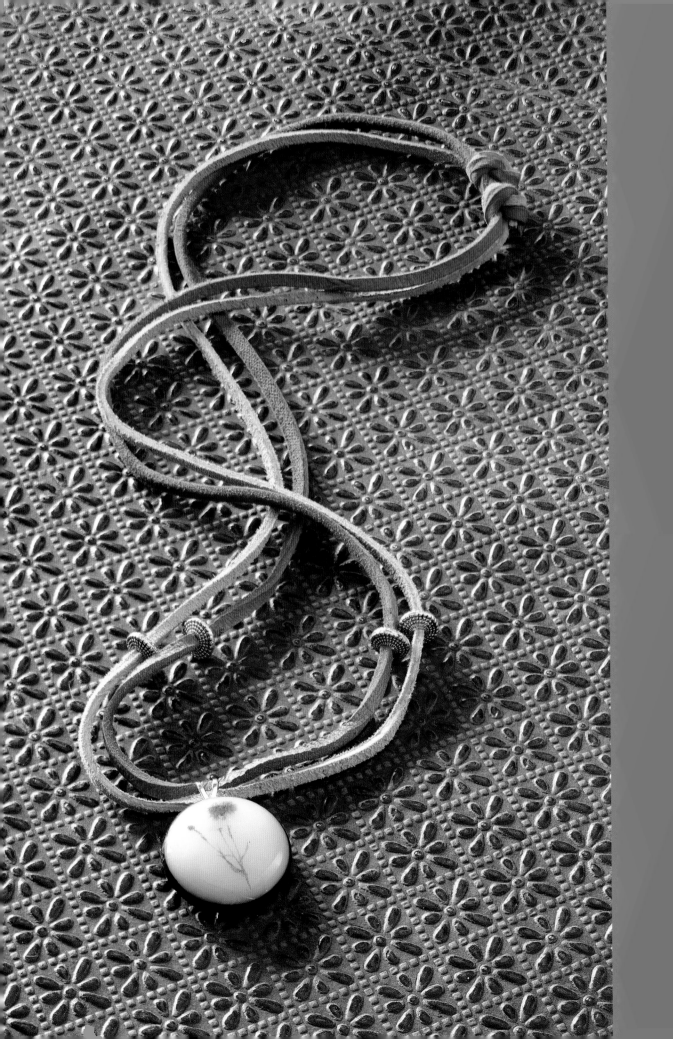

Photo 2

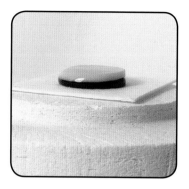

Photo 3

Photo 4

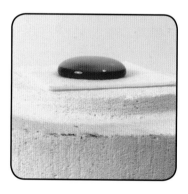

Photo 5

Fused Glass Pendant Necklace continued from page 36.

4. Depending on your microwave, firing times may vary. Pay close attention to the times and note the times in the firing log that is included with the kiln. These are the steps and times I used to fuse the pendant. I used a 1200W microwave, set on HIGH. Follow these steps and when you reach the deep red, glistening shine stage (shown in Photo 5), go to Step 5, the annealing stage.

Note: In the following photos, the kiln cover has been completely removed so that you can see the glass pieces clearly. When you are fusing your pendant, lift the kiln cover enough to see the results and then quickly replace the cover to prevent the hot air from escaping the kiln.

- First Fusing Time: 3¹⁄₂ minutes. Remove the kiln from the microwave, place on the brick, and lift the cover quickly. Notice the uneven edge; the glass is not fused completely **(Photo 2)**. If you see similar results, continue fusing.
- Additional Fusing Time: 30 seconds. Remove the kiln from the microwave, place on the brick, and lift the cover quickly. The edges have become more rounded, but glass is still not fused completely **(Photo 3)**. If you see similar results, continue fusing.
- Additional Fusing Time: 1 minute. Remove the kiln from the microwave, place on the brick, and lift the cover quickly. The glass has become red and the edges are more rounded and even **(Photo 4)**. It's almost done. If you see similar results, continue fusing.
- Additional Fusing Time: 30 seconds. Remove the kiln from the microwave, place on the brick, and lift the cover quickly. The glass is now a deeper red and has a glistening shine; the surface is even and the edges are rounded **(Photo 5)**. This is a good result. Promptly close the cover and allow the glass to anneal.

5. As the glass heats up during the fusing process, the molecules rapidly expand and the glass takes a flowing state. As the kiln temperature gradually drops, annealing takes place, allowing the molecules to settle down and the glass to become solid again. It's important to keep the cover on the kiln until this process is complete. You may be tempted to take a glance but please be patient. Glass that hasn't been properly annealed may develop interior or exterior cracks and may even shatter. Minimum recommendation for annealing (according to the manufacturer's instructions) is at least 30 minutes. I always let it sit at least several hours or even overnight.

6. Once the fused glass is completely cool, cut around the flower decal. Hold the decal in a bowl of water for about 30 seconds. Slide the decal off the paper and place it on the pendant. (Be careful not to flip the image as you slide it off the paper.) Carefully pat with a paper towel to absorb all the moisture. Smooth out the edges and any air bubbles with your fingers. Let dry completely.

7. Place a new square of the kiln paper on the kiln base and place the pendant in the center. Set the kiln in the microwave and replace the cover.

8. Fire for 2 minutes. Take the kiln out of the microwave, place on the brick, and lift the cover quickly. If the image appears to be white, close the kiln, replace in the microwave, and fire 1 more minute. When you see the image appearing and developing color, repeat Step 5 for the annealing process. Once the glass is cool, see if you are happy with the results. If the image still appears white, you can repeat the firing process.

Making the Necklace

1. Place a dot of glue on the front of the round pendant plate. Position the fused glass shape on the plate and press for a few seconds. Let dry for a few hours.

2. Slide the lace pieces through the pendant loop. Thread a bead onto each lace piece. Position the beads about 2"-3" from the pendant.

3. To make the sliding knot closure, take both laces on the left side and place them above the laces on the right. Refer to **Fig. 1** to tie the knots. Trim the excess. Carefully slide the knots toward each other to make the necklace longer. Slide the knots away from each other to make it shorter.

Fig. 1

TUBE PENDANT
NECKLACE

Woven seed beads make a simple, yet striking, tube pendant. Pair the pendant with a stretch cord and you've got a fresh, new necklace.

Skill Level: Intermediate to Advanced

Pendant Size: 2¹/₂" long

Supplies You'll Need
Materials:
- Size 11/0 Japanese cylinder beads in gunmetal black olive
- Size 6/0 seed beads in matte blue green AB
- 3 6mm olive freshwater pearls
- 2 4mm hematite round beads
- 2mm silver metal round bead
- Silver tube bail
- 4mm silver solid ring
- 1.2mm silver crimp tubes
- Silver Stretchiko™ stretch cord
- Beadalon® Wild Fire™ black beading thread .006" dia.
- Aleene's® Jewelry & Metal Glue™

Tools:
- Size 10 beading needle
- Chain-nose pliers
- Flat-nose pliers
- Sharp scissors
- Thread burner

Refer to General Instructions (pages 82-89) and Beadwork Techniques (pages 90-91) before beginning.

Continued on page 42.

Tube Pendant Necklace continued from page 40.

Instructions
Making the Woven Bead Tube

1. Thread the needle with a comfortable length of beading thread and attach an anchor bead.

2. Pick up a sequence of 8 blue green seed beads with a gunmetal black olive cylinder bead between each. This is Column A.

3. Repeat Step 2 to make Column B.

4. Arrange the columns so they are side by side. Pass the needle back through Column A **(Photo 1)**.

5. Pass the needle through the 1st seed bead on Column B, pass the needle back through the 1st seed bead on Column A, and pass the needle through the 1st seed bead on Column B again **(Fig. 1)**. Pass the needle through the cylinder bead and the 2nd seed bead on Column B.

6. Pass the needle through the 2nd seed bead and 1st cylinder bead on Column A; pass the needle through the 2nd seed bead, the next cylinder bead, and the 3rd seed bead on Column B.

7. Continue this pattern to connect Columns A and B. (At the end, remove the anchor bead and tie 3 half hitch knots with the tail and the working thread.) Pass the needle through either column to come out on the other end of the beadwork.

Photo 1

Fig. 1

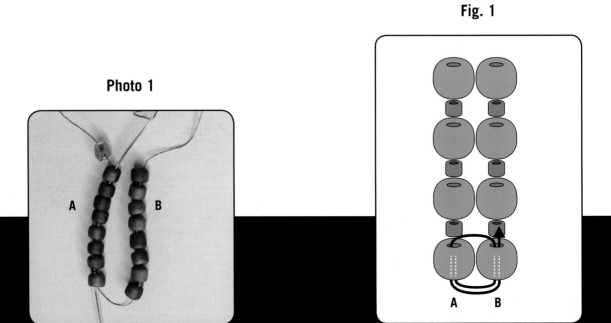

8. Pick up another sequence of seed beads and cylinder beads for Column C. Arrange Column C alongside Columns A and B. Pass the needle through Column B *(Photo 2)*.

9. Repeat Steps 5-7 to attach Column C to Column B. Tie 3 half hitch knots. Now there are 3 Columns attached to each other.

10. Pass the needle through Column B. Pick up another sequence of seed beads and cylinder beads for Column D. Pass back through Column B to bring Column D on top of the first 3 columns *(Photo 3)*.

11. Repeat Steps 5-7 to attach Column D to Column B. Tie 3 half hitch knots.

12. Pass the needle through the column on one side of Column B. Pick up the beads and attach Column E as you did the other columns. Repeat to attach Column F to the column on the other side of Column B.

13. Attach Column E and Column F to each other to finish the bead tube. Secure and end the thread.

Continued on page 44.

Photo 2

Photo 3

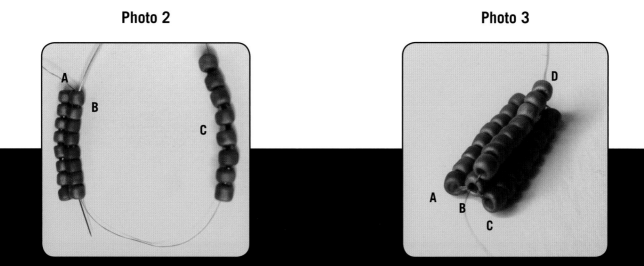

Tube Pendant Necklace continued from page 43.

Making the Necklace

1. To make the pendant, thread the needle with a comfortable length of beading thread. Pass the needle through any column on the bead tube. Pick up a pearl, a crimp tube, a hematite bead, a crimp tube, a pearl, and the silver bead. Skip the silver bead and pass the needle back through all the beads, passing through a different column on the bead tube. Tie 3 half hitch knots.

2. Pick up a pearl, a crimp tube, a hematite bead, and the solid ring. Pass the needle back through all the beads, choosing a different column to pass the needle through on the bead tube. Repeat 3-4 more times to attach the beads securely, stopping at the place where you started. Tie 3 half hitch knots and end the thread.

3. Open the ring on the tube bail and attach the pendant. Close the ring.

4. Cut the desired length of Stretchiko™ cord. Use the beading needle to gently push the cord through the tube bail. Seal the cord ends with the thread burner to prevent fraying. Put a small amount of glue on the cord ends and bring together. Hold for a minute or so until the glue begins to dry. Set aside, making sure the cord ends stay together; let dry overnight. Slide the tube over the glued area.

BEADED PILLOWS BRACELET

These beaded pillow beads are quite unique and fun to make. Multiple bead sequences means the bracelet size can be easily adjusted. The bead amounts given in the Materials list are what I used for a 7³/₈" long bracelet, excluding the clasp.

Skill Level: Intermediate to Advanced

Supplies You'll Need
Materials:
- Size 11/0 Japanese cylinder beads in gun metal olive (I used about 600 beads to make 3 pillow beads)
- Size 11/0 Japanese cylinder beads in silver lined caramel (I used about 200 beads to make a pillow bead)
- Size 11/0 Japanese cylinder beads in silver lined chocolate (I used about 200 beads to make a pillow bead)
- Size 6/0 glass seed beads in colors to match the Japanese cylinder beads (these are strung inside the pillow beads)
- 8 4mm light rose AB crystal bicone beads
- 4 6mm copper crystal round beads
- 2 10mm x 14mm silver corrugated rondelle beads
- 8 6mm x 10mm silver corrugated rondelle beads
- Silver crimp tubes
- Silver toggle clasp with attached jump ring
- 2 4mm silver solid rings
- 49 strand nylon-coated silver stringing wire .018" dia.
- Beadalon® Wild Fire™ black beading thread .006" dia.

Tools:
- Size 12 beading needle
- Chain-nose pliers
- Flat-nose pliers
- Crimping pliers
- Wire cutters
- Sharp scissors

Continued on page 46.

Beaded Pillows Bracelet continued from page 45.

Refer to General Instructions (pages 82-89) and Beadwork Techniques (pages 90-91) before beginning.

Instructions
Making the Beaded Pillow Beads

1. Thread the needle with a comfortable length of beading thread and attach an anchor bead. For the pillow bead, pick up 3 Japanese cylinder beads for your 1st row (Row 1A).

2. Pick up 3 more cylinder beads and pass the needle back through the 3 beads on 1st row (Row 1A). Pass the needle through 3 beads on the 2nd row (Row 2A) *(Fig. 1)*. Continue this pattern until you have 9 rows.

3. Pass the needle back through all the rows to return to the 1st row (Row 1A) *(Fig. 2)*.

4. Pick up 14 cylinder beads. Skip the last 3 beads strung and pass the needle back through the next 3 beads on the thread; this forms Rows 1B and 2B. Pass the needle through 3 beads on Row 2B *(Fig. 3)*.

Continued on page 48.

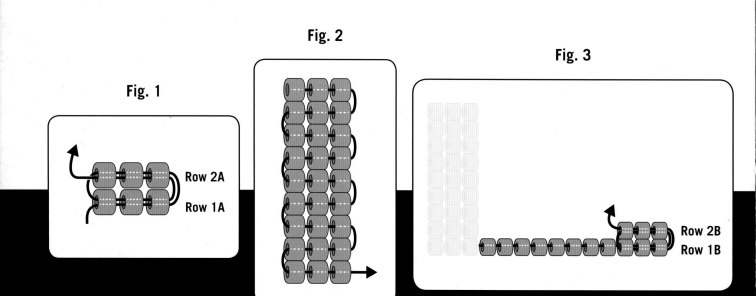

Fig. 2

Fig. 3

Fig. 1

Row 2A

Row 1A

Row 2B

Row 1B

Beaded Pillows Bracelet continued from page 46.

Fig. 4

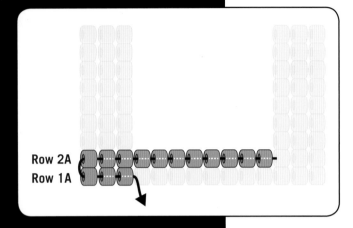

Row 2A
Row 1A

Fig. 5

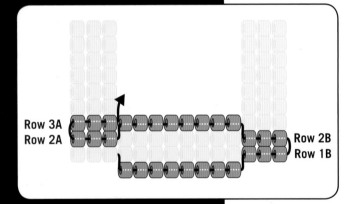

Row 3A
Row 2A

Row 2B
Row 1B

5. Pick up 3 cylinder beads and referring to **Fig. 1**, **page 46**, pass the needle back through the 3 beads on Row 2B. Pass the needle through 3 beads on the 3rd row (Row 3B). Continue this pattern until you have 9 rows. Referring to **Fig. 2**, **page 46**, pass the needle back through all the rows to return to the 2nd row (Row 2B).

6. Pick up 8 cylinder beads and pass the needle through Row 2A on the opposite side. Pass the needle through 3 beads on Row 1A *(Fig. 4)*.

7. Pick up 8 cylinder beads and pass the needle through Row 1B on the opposite side. Now there are 2 strands of 8 beads connecting both Row 1's. Pass the needle through 3 beads on Row 2B. Pick up 8 beads and pass the needle through the Row 2A on the opposite side. Pass the needle through 3 beads on Row 3A *(Fig. 5)*.

8. Continue working in this manner to connect sides A and B with 2 strands of 8 cylinder beads per row. Secure and end the thread.

9. Make as many pillow beads as you'd like for the bracelet. I made 3 gunmetal olive pillow beads, 1 silver lined caramel pillow bead, and 1 silver lined chocolate pillow bead for my 7³/₈" long bracelet (excluding the clasp).

Making the Bracelet

1. To determine the size of your bracelet: Measure your wrist slightly below the wrist bone. Add 1"-1¹/₂" for wearing ease, depending on how loose you like wearing bracelets. Measure the size of the closed clasp and subtract that.

For example: My wrist is 6". I like my bracelets a bit loose, and my closed clasp is 1".
Here's the math:
   6" + 1¹/₂" = 7¹/₂"
   (wrist size + wearing ease)
   7¹/₂" – 1" = 6¹/₂" is my bracelet size
   (determined measurement – clasp size)

2. Using the wire cutters, cut a length of stringing wire the bracelet size plus 2". Attach a solid jump ring to one end.

3. String the following bead sequences on the wire:
Sequence #1:
  • small corrugated rondelle bead
  • 5 gunmetal olive seed beads
  • slide the gunmetal olive pillow bead on, covering the seed beads *(Photo 1)*
  • small corrugated rondelle bead

Sequence #2:
  • light rose bicone bead
  • copper round bead
  • light rose bicone bead

Sequence #3: Repeat Sequence #1 with the silver lined chocolate seed beads and beaded pillow bead

Sequence #4: Repeat Sequence #2

Sequence #5: Repeat Sequence #1 with the large corrugated rondelle beads

Sequence #6: Repeat Sequence #2

Sequence #7: Repeat Sequence #1 with the silver lined caramel seed beads and beaded pillow bead

Sequence #8: Repeat Sequence #2

Sequence #9: Repeat Sequence #1

4. Finish the remaining wire end with a solid ring. Attach the clasp.

Photo 1

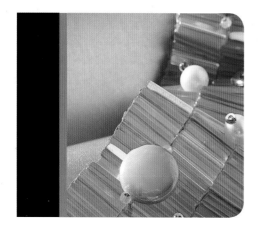

TANGERINE AQUA DOTS BRACELET

This square stitch bugle bead bracelet is accented with beads in a variety of styles and colors.

Skill Level: Intermediate to Advanced

Supplies You'll Need
Materials:
- 3mm x 11mm tangerine AB bugle beads (I used 184 beads for for my 7" long bracelet, excluding the clasp).
- Size 11/0 seed beads in dark blue and lemon yellow
- 6mm lemon yellow pearls (I used 8 pearls)
- 12mm hematite black flat disc beads with center drilled holes (I used 4 beads)
- 6mm milky aqua blue lentil beads with top drilled holes (I used 4 beads)
- 11mm aqua disc shell beads with side drilled holes (I used 3 beads)
- 4mm silver split rings
- 6mm silver jump rings
- 1" silver head pin
- 3 12mm silver solid rings
- Silver lobster clasp with attached jump ring
- Beadalon® Wild Fire™ black beading thread .006" dia.

Tools:
- Size 12 beading needle
- Flat-nose pliers
- Chain-nose pliers
- Round-nose pliers
- Wire cutters
- Bead mat

Continued on page 52.

Tangerine Aqua Dots Bracelet continued from page 50.

Refer to General Instructions (pages 82-89) and Beadwork Techniques (pages 90-91 and 94) before beginning.

Instructions

1. Thread the needle with a comfortable length of beading thread and attach an anchor bead.

2. Pick up 2 bugle beads, a split ring and 2 bugle beads to begin working Square Stitch. Work Square Stitch (page 94), picking up 1 bead at a time, until you have 45 rows or the bracelet is 1 row short of the desired length. *(Keep in mind that the 1³/₄" extension chain will be added to the bracelet to make it adjustable.)* For the last row, pick up 2 bugle beads, a split ring, and 2 bugle beads. Tie 3 half hitch knots and pass the needle back through all the rows (page 94). Secure and end the thread.

3. Draw around the outer edges of the woven bracelet on paper. This will be the Design Diagram.

4. Place the woven bracelet on the bead mat. Arrange the seed beads, pearls, disc beads, lentil beads, and shell beads as desired. Keep the pattern interesting by varying the distance between beads and placing similar shapes further apart. Once you are happy with the design, transfer it bead by bead onto the Design Diagram.

5. Thread the needle with a comfortable length of beading thread. Secure the thread and pass the needle through the beadwork to make your way to the desired bead location. Attach all the beads as shown on your Design Diagram, using the methods on page 53. Once all beads are attached, secure and end the thread.

Fig. 1

Pearls and seed beads: Come out with your thread. Pick up a pearl and a seed bead. Pass the needle back through the pearl and the bugle bead you came out of on the woven bracelet; move on to attach the next bead *(Fig. 1)*.

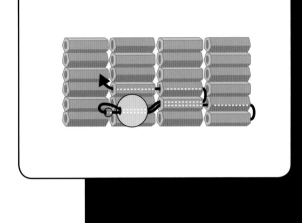

Discs with side drilled holes and seed beads: Come out with your thread. Pick up a seed bead, a disc shell bead, and another seed bead. Lay the bead sequence on the woven bracelet and pass the needle through the closest bugle bead on your beadwork; move on to attach the next bead *(Fig. 2)*. *(Do not pull the thread too tight, as this will cause the beadwork to bulge.)*

Fig. 2

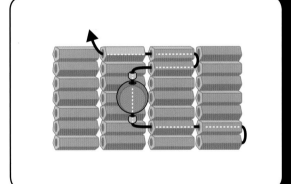

Discs with center drilled holes and lentil beads: Come out with your thread. Pick up a flat disc bead, a lentil bead, and a seed bead. Pass the needle back through the lentil bead, the disc bead, and the bugle bead you came out of on your woven bracelet; move on to attach the next bead *(Fig. 3)*.

Continued on page 54.

Fig. 3

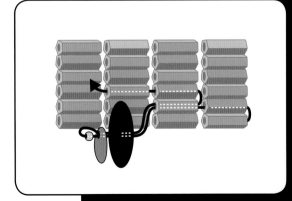

Tangerine Aqua Dots Bracelet continued from page 53.

6. For the pearl dangle on the extension chain, slide a pearl onto a head pin and use the round-nose pliers to wrap the head pin around until it crosses itself *(Photo 1)*.

7. Slide the open loop of the dangle onto a solid ring. Holding the ring and the loop with flat-nose pliers, make a wrapped loop *(Photo 2)*. Trim any excess wire. Attach a jump ring to the solid ring.

8. Attach 2 jump rings each to the remaining solid rings. Attach the jump rings to each other to complete the extension chain. Attach the extension chain to one split ring on the bracelet.

9. Attach the lobster clasp to the remaining split ring on the opposite side of the bracelet.

Photo 1

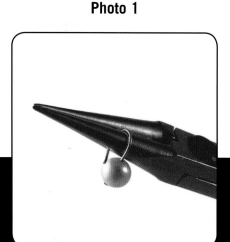

Photo 2

WOVEN PENDANT NECKLACE

It's not hard to weave a pendant following a Square Stitch chart. If you'd like to design your own pendant, we've included blank Square Stitch grids on page 95.

Skill Level: Intermediate to Advanced

Pendant Size: 1" x ⁷/₈"

Supplies You'll Need
Materials:
- Size 11/0 Japanese cylinder beads in light blue and matte brown
- 15mm blue shell loop bead
- 5mm x 7mm brown freshwater pearl
- 2mm silver metal round bead
- Silver tube bail
- 2 silver crimp tubes with loop ends
- Silver lobster clasp with attached jump ring
- Black 2mm leather cord
- Beadalon® Wild Fire™ black beading thread .006" dia.

Tools:
- Size 12 beading needle
- Chain-nose pliers
- Flat-nose pliers

Refer to General Instructions (pages 82-89) and Beadwork Techniques (pages 90-91 and 94) before beginning.

Continued on page 56.

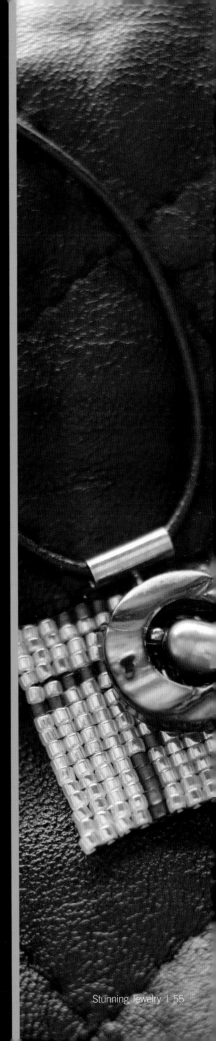

Woven Pendant on Leather Necklace continued from page 55.

Instructions

1. To make the woven pendant, thread the needle with a comfortable length of beading thread and attach an anchor bead. Referring to the Chart below, pick up the bottom row of cylinder beads to begin working Square Stitch (page 94). Work Square Stitch, picking up 2 beads at a time and following the Chart for color changes to complete the woven pendant.

2. Place the shell loop bead on the pendant. Pass the needle through the beads of the pendant to a spot near one of the holes on the shell bead. Pass the needle through 2 beads at a time. When you need to change direction, make a U-turn and go to the next row *(Fig. 1)*. Make sure the thread stays hidden inside the beadwork.

3. Once you are at the desired spot on the pendant, pass the needle through the hole on the shell bead, pick up the silver bead and the pearl, and pass the needle through the opposite hole on the shell bead. Pass the needle through the 2 closest cylinder beads. Make sure not to pull the thread too tight.

4. Pass the needle through several cylinder beads to turn around. Pass the needle through the shell bead, pearl, and silver bead again. Pass the needle through a few cylinder beads to turn around again. Repeat a few times, so that the shell bead, pearl, and silver bead are securely attached to the pendant. Secure and end the thread.

5. Open the ring on the tube bail and slide it between 2 beads at the top center of the woven piece; close the ring around the threads.

6. Cut the desired length of leather cord. Slide on the woven pendant. Finish the cord ends and attach the clasp.

Chart

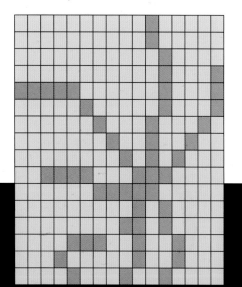

Fig. 1

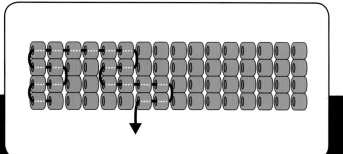

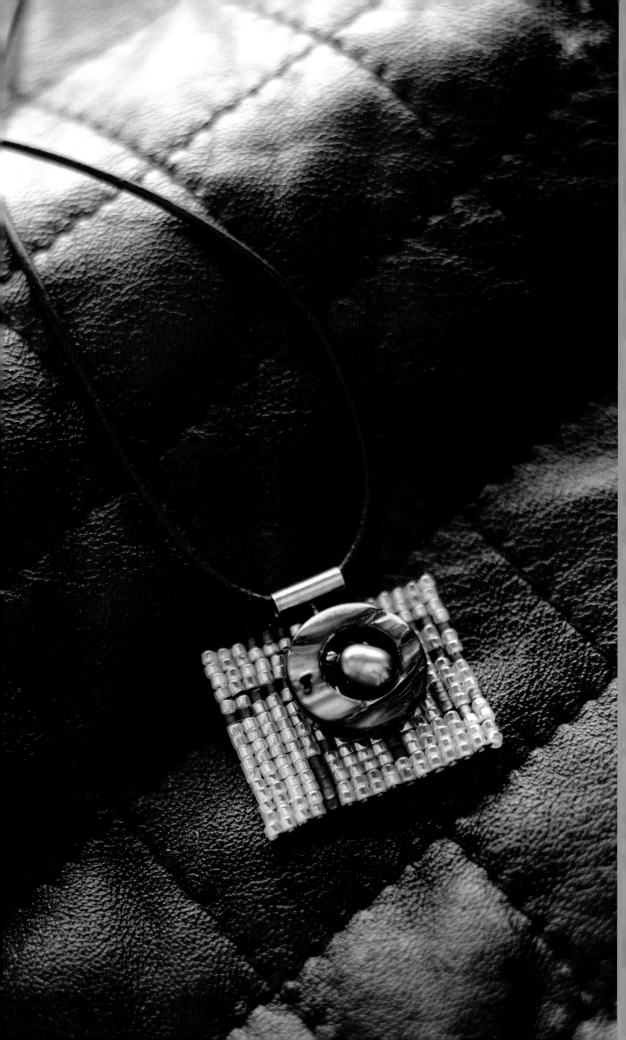

DANGLES BRACELET

This sparkly, flirty bracelet begins with a Peyote Stitch base that is then embellished with a medley of coordinating beads. I like this bracelet so much that I made 2 alternate versions (shown on page 60). The process is the same; I just used different beads.

Skill Level: Intermediate to Advanced

Supplies You'll Need
Materials:
• Size 11/0 Japanese cylinder beads in dark amethyst
• Size 6/0 seed beads in matte plum iris
• Glass beads in assorted shapes, sizes, and colors for dangles (I used 4mm and 6mm fire-polished faceted round beads, 4mm x 6mm teardrop beads, 3mm x 11mm dagger beads, and 4mm round beads in amethyst, alexandrite, and purple)
• Silver magnetic clasp
• 2 silver bead caps
• Beadalon® Wild Fire™ black beading thread .006" dia.

Tools:
• Size 10 beading needle
• Chain-nose pliers
• Flat-nose pliers
• Sharp scissors

Continued on page 60.

Dangles Bracelet continued from page 58.

Refer to General Instructions (pages 82-89) and Beadwork Techniques (pages 90-93) before beginning.

Instructions

1. To determine the size of your bracelet: Measure your wrist slightly below the wrist bone. Add 1"-1^1/$_2$" for wearing ease, depending on how loose you like wearing bracelets. Measure the size of the closed clasp and subtract that.

For example: My wrist is 6". I like my bracelets a bit loose, and my closed clasp is 1".
Here's the math:

> *6" + 1^1/$_2$" = 7^1/$_2$"*
> *(wrist size + wearing ease)*
> *7^1/$_2$" – 1" = 6^1/$_2$" is my bracelet size*
> *(determined measurement – clasp size)*

2. Thread the needle with a comfortable length of beading thread and attach an anchor bead.

3. Pick up 2 seed beads to begin working Peyote Stitch (page 93). Continue to work Peyote Stitch until the bracelet base is the determined bracelet size. Add or reduce the number of rows to be an even number of beads on each side.

More ideas for Dangles Bracelets

4. Reinforce the end portion of the bracelet base by passing the needle through the last 4 beads 3 times *(Fig. 1)*.

5. To embellish the bracelet base, pass the needle through the seed bead on the second row and pick up 2 cylinder beads, any assorted bead, and a cylinder bead. Skip the top cylinder bead and pass the needle back through the assorted bead and the 2 cylinder beads. Pass the needle through the same bead on the base *(Fig. 2)*.

6. Repeat Step 5 to add another embellishment to the same seed bead, but on the opposite side.

7. Repeat Step 5 to add embellishments to both sides of all but the last row of the bracelet base *(Fig. 3)*. End the thread.

8. Thread the needle with a comfortable length of beading thread. Secure the thread and pass the needle through the 2 beads on Row 1 and Row 2. Pass the needle through 1 bead on Row 1, through a bead cap, through a clasp half, back through the bead cap, and through the next bead on Row 1. Pass the needle through the 2 beads on Row 2. Repeat a few times, until the clasp half is securely attached to the beadwork. Secure and end the thread. Repeat on the opposite end.

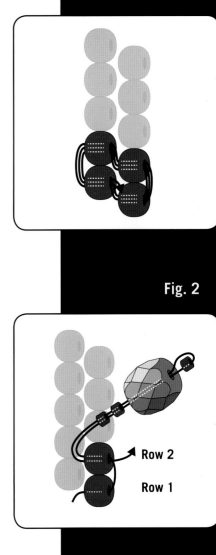

Fig. 1

Fig. 2

Row 2

Row 1

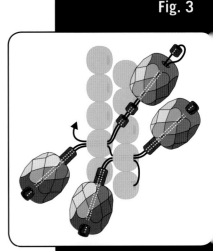

Fig. 3

FUZZY BEAD FUR BRACELET

A bead core with lots of "fuzzy bead fur" is a distinctive and fashionable look for your wrist.

Skill Level: Intermediate to Advanced

Supplies You'll Need
Materials:
- Size 6/0 seed beads in matte blue olive AB (I used about 1150 beads for my 7¾" bracelet, excluding the clasp)
- Size 11/0 Japanese cylinder beads in gunmetal blue olive (I used about 385 beads)
- Silver magnetic tube clasp
- Beadalon® Wild Fire™ black beading thread .006" dia.

Tools:
- Size 10 beading needle
- Sharp scissors

Refer to General Instructions (pages 82-89) before beginning.

Continued on page 64.

Fuzzy Bead Fur Bracelet Continued from page 62.

Instructions

If you find it hard to see the core beads, try using a different color seed bead the first time you make this bracelet.

1. Thread the needle with a comfortable length of beading thread and attach an anchor bead, leaving an 8" tail.

2. Pick up seed beads for the core of your bracelet. Make the core long enough to wrap around your wrist, adding about 1½"-2" for the thickness of the bracelet.

3. Pick up 1 more seed bead and pass the needle back through the last bead on the core **(Photo 1)**.

4. To embellish the core beads, pick up 3 seed beads and 1 cylinder bead. Skip the cylinder bead and pass the needle back through the 3 seed beads. Pass the needle through the same seed bead on the core **(Photo 2)**.

5. Repeat Step 4 to add 5 more embellishments to that same 1st core bead **(Photo 3)**.

6. Pass the needle through the 2nd bead on the core and repeat Step 4 to add 6 embellishments to that bead. Continue adding embellishments to each core bead, leaving the last core bead unembellished.

Photo 1

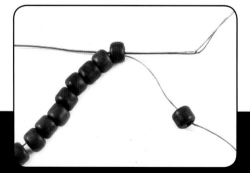

Photo 2

Photo 3

7. Remove the anchor bead and tie 3 half hitch knots with working thread and the tail. Attach one end of the clasp by passing the needle (with the working thread) through the loops on the clasp and the end core beads several times. Tie 3 half hitch knots and trim the excess thread. Repeat on the opposite end of the bracelet.

Tip: You may find it hard to get to the core beads, as the embellishment beads can get in the way. Slide the anchor bead to create about $1/2$" of loose thread, so you can slide the beads to the side temporarily (Photo 4). Make sure to close the gap between the bead you are embellishing and the rest of the beadwork, so your bracelet doesn't become loose.

Photo 4

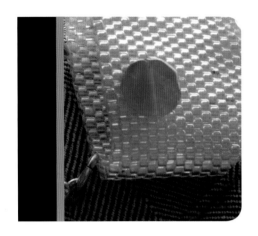

SECRET AMULET POCKET PENDANT NECKLACE

A simple leather cord allows this Peyote Stitch amulet pocket pendant to be in the spotlight.

Skill Level: Intermediate to Advanced

Pendant Size: 1³/₈" square

Supplies You'll Need
Materials:
- Size 11/0 Japanese cylinder beads in transparent aqua AB (I used about 1000 beads)
- 6mm carnelian gemstone disc bead
- 3 4mm transparent amber glass round beads
- 5 silver metal spacer beads with a 2mm hole
- 2 6mm x 7.5mm silver oval jump rings
- 2 silver crimp tubes with loop ends
- Silver lobster clasp with attached jump ring
- 2mm brown leather cord
- Beadalon® Wild Fire™ clear beading thread .006" dia.

Tools:
- Size 12 beading needle
- Chain-nose pliers
- Flat-nose pliers
- Sharp scissors

Refer to General Instructions (pages 82-89) and Beadwork Techniques (pages 90-93) before beginning.

Continued on page 68.

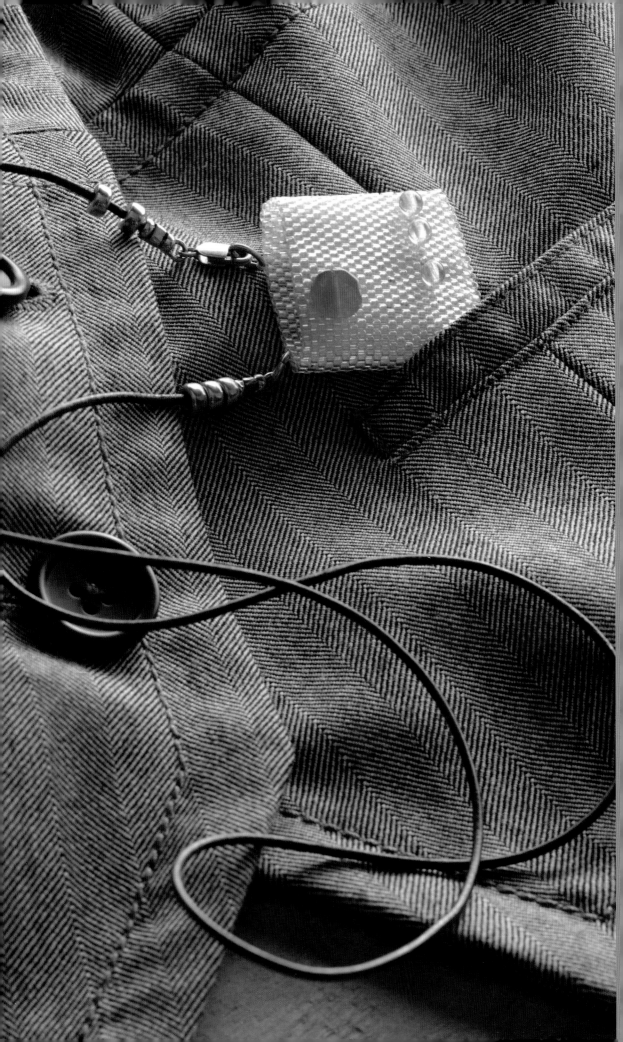

Secret Amulet Pocket Pendant Necklace continued from page 66.

Instructions
Making the Peyote Stitch Pocket

1. Thread the needle with a comfortable length of beading thread and attach an anchor bead. Pick up 24 cylinder beads to begin working Peyote Stitch (pages 92-93). Work Peyote Stitch for 80 rows.

2. Fold the beadwork into a tube and connect the end beads in a zigzag pattern **(Fig. 1)**. Remove the anchor bead and tie 3 half hitch knots with the working thread and the beginning tail. Secure and end the beginning tail.

3. Closing the tube bottom will create the pocket. Pass the needle through the beadwork, securing the thread along the way and coming out the end bead on Row 2A. Refer to **Figs. 2 and 3** to pick up cylinder beads and join the A rows and B rows.

Fig. 1

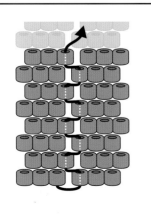

Fig. 2

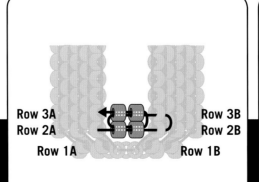

Fig. 3

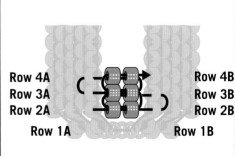

4. Place the carnelian gemstone on the pocket. Pass the needle through the beadwork until it is near the gemstone.

5. Come out with your needle, pick up the gemstone, and pass the needle through the bead closest to the gemstone. *(Do not pull the thread too tight, as this will cause the beadwork to bulge.)* Pass the needle through the beadwork on the pocket to make a turn around *(Fig. 3)*. Repeat a few times to securely attach the gemstone to the pocket.

6. Repeat Step 5 to attach the 3 amber beads.

7. To attach the oval jump rings to the pocket, come out along the top back edge with the needle about ¼" from one side edge. Pick up a jump ring and pass the needle back into the beadwork *(Fig. 4)*. Repeat 3-4 times to securely attach the jump ring. Pass the needle through the beads to the position of the second ring and repeat to attach the remaining ring. Secure and end the thread.

8. Cut the desired length of cord. Slide on 5 silver beads. Attach the cord ends. Attach the clasp to one cord end.

Fig. 3

Fig. 4

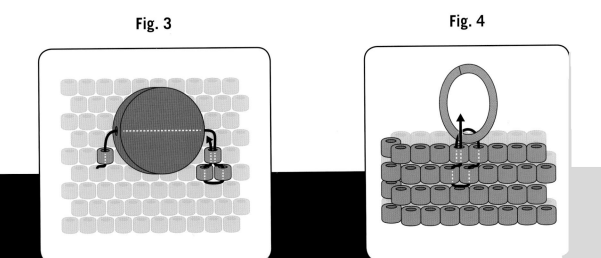

SEA CUCUMBER BRACELET

Beads, head pins, and Katiedids™ components come together to create a custom toggle-style clasp in this unusual bracelet inspired by the aquatic sea cucumber. This bracelet is very thick, so I've added a bit more wearing ease to the length.

Skill Level: Intermediate to Advanced

Supplies You'll Need
Materials:
- Size 6/0 glass sead beads in matte plum (approx 100-120)
- Size 11/0 glass sead beads in silver lined bright pink (approx 94-114)
- 12mm hematite black flat disc beads with center drilled holes (approx 80-100)
- 10mm pink AB flat disc shell beads with side drilled holes (approx 80-100)
- 5 6mm silver rondelle beads
- 1 package Beadalon® Katiedids™ silver 25mm round hole components
- 2 4mm silver split rings
- 2 4mm silver jump rings
- 2 6mm x 7.5mm silver oval jump rings
- 5 2" silver head pins with ball heads
- Beadalon® silver 3.4mm elongated cable chain
- Beadalon® Wild Fire™ black beading thread .006" dia.

Tools:
- Size 10 beading needle
- Chain-nose pliers
- Flat-nose pliers
- Round-nose pliers
- Wire cutters

Continued on page 72.

Sea Cucumber Bracelet continued from page 70.

Refer to General Instructions (pages 82-89) and Beadwork Techniques (pages 90-91 and 94) before beginning.

Instructions
Weaving and Beading the Bracelet

1. Thread the needle with a comfortable length of beading thread and attach an anchor bead. Pick up 2 plum seed beads and begin weaving a base for your bracelet using Square Stitch (page 94). Continue the Square Stitch until the woven base is long enough to wrap around your wrist comfortably, adding 1" for the thickness of the bracelet.

2. Remove the anchor bead and tie 3 half hitch knots with the working thread and beginning tail. Secure and end the tail. Pass the needle with the working thread through the last 2 beads of the woven base. This is Row 1.

3. To bead the bracelet, pick up a pink disc bead, a black disc bead, and a bright pink seed bead. Skip the seed bead and pass the needle back through the black and pink disc beads. Pass the needle back through Row 1 *(Fig. 1)*.

4. Repeat Step 3 on the opposite side of Row 1. Pass the needle through Row 2.

5. Repeat Steps 3 and 4 until all of the woven base rows have been beaded.

6. Pass the needle through 1 bead on the last row and pick up a split ring, pass the needle through the next bead on that row. Pass the needle through 2 beads on the next row down. Repeat a few times to secure the ring to the woven base. Secure and end the thread. Repeat on the opposite end of the bracelet.

Fig. 1

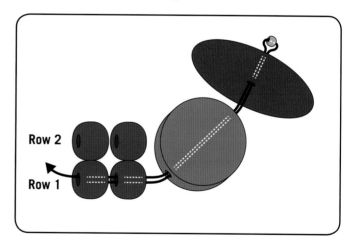

Row 2

Row 1

Making the Toggle Clasp

1. To make the bar, pick up a sequence of 5 plum seed beads with a silver rondelle bead between each on a head pin. Insert another head pin through the beads from the opposite side. Leaving about $^1/_8$" between the last bead and the ball end of the head pin, bend each head pin end at a 90° angle *(Photo 1)*.

Photo 1

2. Wrap the bent wire end around the head pin 2 or 3 times on each side *(Photo 2)*. Trim any excess wire.

3. Attach an oval jump ring to the right and left of the center plum bead.

Photo 2

4. Attach one end of a 1" chain length to both jump rings. Attach the opposite end to the split ring on one bracelet end.

5. To make the ring, slide a head pin through one side of the round component and make a wrapped loop *(Photo 3)*. Repeat on the other side.

6. Pick up a sequence of 7 plum beads with a bright pink bead between each on a 6" length of beading thread. Place inside the component. Pass the thread under the head pin and pick up the same bead sequence for the other side. Pass the thread under the head pin and tie 3 half hitch knots to secure. Trim the excess thread.

Photo 3

7. To create the dangle, pick up a plum bead and a rondelle bead on a head pin and make a large wrapped loop. Attach the dangle to one end of the ring component with a jump ring.

8. Attach the ring component to the remaining split ring on the bracelet with a jump ring.

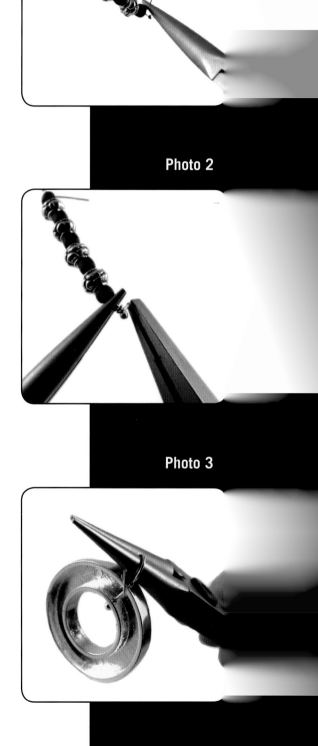

CHOCOLATE DANCE PENDANT NECKLACE

Step out onto the dance floor with a chocolate colored Peyote Stitch bead tube that is dripping with shiny beads.

Skill Level: Intermediate to Advanced

Pendant Size: 1 $^{13}/_{16}$" x $^{13}/_{16}$"

Supplies You'll Need
Materials:
- Size 11/0 Japanese cylinder beads in dark brown AB (approx 960 beads)
- Glass beads in assorted shapes, sizes, and colors for dangles (I used 4mm and 6mm smooth round beads, 4mm and 6mm faceted round beads, and 3mm x 11mm dagger beads in pink, rose, dark brown, topaz, amber, and silver quartz)
- 1" silver head pins
- 4mm silver jump rings
- Beadalon® Wild Fire™ black beading thread .006" dia.
- Brown 2 mm leather cord
- 2 silver crimp tubes with loop ends
- Silver lobster clasp with attached jump ring

Tools:
- Size 12 beading needle
- Chain-nose pliers
- Flat-nose pliers
- Round-nose pliers
- Wire cutters
- Sharp scissors

Refer to General Instructions (pages 82-89) and Beadwork Techniques (pages 90-93) before beginning.

Continued on page 76.

Chocolate Dance Pendant Necklace continued from page 74.

Instructions

Making a Woven Bead Tube

1. Thread the needle with a comfortable length of beading thread and attach an anchor bead.

2. Pick up 36 cylinder beads to begin working Peyote Stitch (pages 92-93). Work Peyote Stitch until you have 4 rows.

3. This woven tube has "top beads," beads that sit on top of the tube through which you later attach bead dangles. To add the first top bead, start the next row by adding 2 beads using Peyote Stitch. Pick up a bead and pass back through the last bead you passed the needle through ***(Fig. 1)***. Slide the bead so it sits on top of the beadwork. This is the top bead.

4. Continue working in Peyote Stitch, working a total of 50 rows and randomly adding about 50-55 top beads. Keep the top beads spaced a few beads apart, both vertically and horizontally ***(Photo 1)***.

5. Fold the woven bead piece into a tube, making sure the top beads are on the outside; connect the end beads in a zigzag pattern ***(Fig. 2)***.

6. Remove the anchor bead and tie 3 half hitch knots with the working thread and the beginning tail; secure and end the threads.

Making and Attaching Dangles

It's easier to make all the dangles at one time and then attach them to the beaded tube. Alternate the shapes, sizes, and colors to make the pattern interesting and vibrant.

1. For beads with center drilled holes, slide the bead onto a head pin and make a loop on top. Open the loop the same way you open a jump ring and slide it through one of the top beads. Close the loop.

2. For beads with side drilled holes, open a jump ring and slide the bead on; don't close the ring yet. When you are ready to attach the dangles, simply put the jump ring through one of the top beads on the beaded tube and close the ring.

Completing the Necklace

1. Cut the desired length of cord. Finish the cord ends (page 89) and attach the clasp. Slide on the Beaded Pendant.

Fig. 1

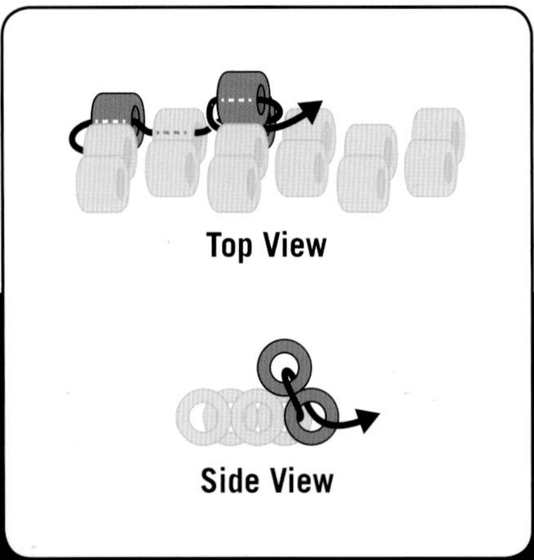

Top View
Side View

Photo 1

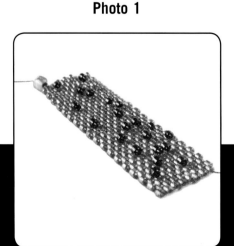

Fig. 2

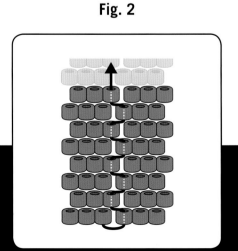

BEADED FLOWER PENDANT NECKLACE

This gorgeous floral pendant is composed of a woven bead center, which is embellished with sparkling dagger beads.

Skill Level: Intermediate to Advanced

Pendant Size: 1³/₄" diameter

Supplies You'll Need
Materials:
- Size 6/0 glass sead beads in matte seafoam AB
- 3mm x 11mm glass dagger beads in matte light green AB and matte black AB
- Size 11/0 glass sead beads in silver lined light olive
- Black 2mm leather cord
- 2 silver crimp tubes with loop ends
- Silver lobster clasp with attached jump ring
- Beadalon® Wild Fire™ black beading thread .006" dia.

Tools:
- Size 12 beading needle
- Chain-nose pliers
- Flat-nose pliers
- Crimp pliers
- Sharp scissors

Refer to General Instructions (pages 82-89) and Beadwork Techniques (pages 90-91) before beginning.

Continued on page 78.

Beaded Flower Pendant Necklace continued from page 77.

Instructions
Weaving the Base Circle

1. Thread the needle with a comfortable length of beading thread. String on 3 size 6/0 seed beads. Leaving a 6" tail, tie 2 half hitch knots to create a triangle *(Fig. 1)*. Pass the needle through the first bead *(Photo 1)*.

2. Pick up a bead and pass the needle through the next bead of the triangle *(Photo 2)*. Repeat twice. Pass the needle through the next bead *(Photo 3)*.

Continued on page 80.

Fig. 1

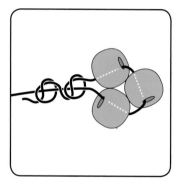

Photo 1

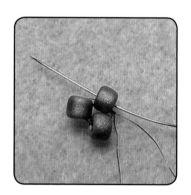

Photo 2

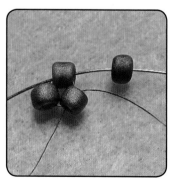

Photo 3

Beaded Flower Pendant Necklace continued from page 78.

3. Pick up 2 beads, skip a bead, and pass the needle through the next bead. Repeat twice. Pass the needle through the next 2 beads *(Fig. 2)*.

4. ★ Pick up 2 beads, skip a bead, and pass the needle through the next bead. Pick up a bead and pass the needle through the next bead. Repeat from ★ twice. Pass the needle through the next 2 beads *(Fig. 3)*.

5. ★ Pick up a bead, skip a bead, and pass the needle through the next bead. Pick up a bead, skip a bead, and pass the needle through the next 2 beads. Repeat from ★ twice. Pass the needle through the next bead *(Fig. 4)*.

6. ★ Pick up 2 beads, skip a bead, and pass the needle through the next bead. Pick up a bead, skip 2 beads, and pass the needle through the next bead. Repeat from ★ twice. Pass the needle through the next 2 beads *(Fig. 5)*.

7. ★ Pick up a bead, skip a bead, and pass the needle through the next bead. Pick up 2 beads, skip a bead and pass the needle through the next 2 beads. Repeat from ★ twice *(Fig. 6)*. Pass the needle through all 18 beads on the outer ring of the circle, pulling the thread a bit tight, causing the circle to cup slightly. Secure the thread.

Fig. 2

Fig. 3

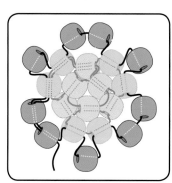

Fig. 4

Fig. 5

Fig. 6

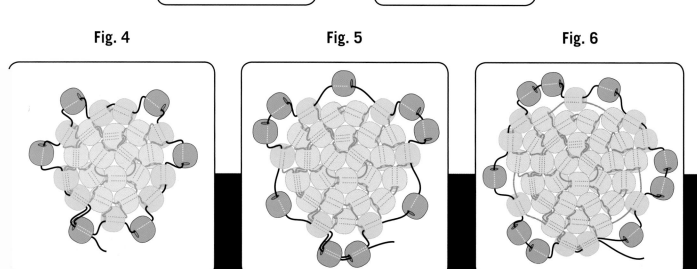

Embellishing the Base Circle

When embellishing, randomly choose the dagger bead colors to keep the pattern more interesting.

1. You can start embellishing at any bead on the outer ring of your base circle. Pass the needle through the chosen bead, pick up 2 size 11/0 seed beads and 1 dagger bead, pass the needle back through the 2 seed beads *(Photo 4)*. Pass the needle back through the bead on the base circle and repeat the embellishment on the other side of that bead *(Fig. 7)*.

2. Embellish every other bead on the outer ring of the base circle *(Photo 5)*. Continue embellishing the remaining base circle beads until you reach the last 3 beads in the middle.

3. Pass the needle through 1 of the last 3 middle beads; pick up 3 size 11/0 seed beads, skip the last seed bead picked up, and pass the needle back through the first 2 seed beads. Repeat this embellishment on each side of the remaining 2 beads of the base circle. Secure and end the thread.

4. Run a length of leather cord through 2 adjacent beads on the outer ring of the base circle. Finish the cord ends (page 89) and attach the clasp.

Photo 4

Fig. 7

Photo 5

GENERAL INSTRUCTIONS

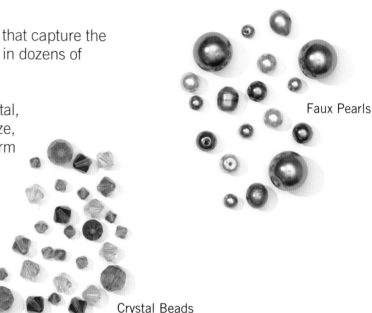

Ceramic Beads

BEADS

Beads come in all sizes, shapes, colors, finishes, and materials. Most of the beads I've used are glass; but even within the glass beads, there are numerous types: seed beads, glass pearls, and dagger beads, just to name a few. There are also crystal beads, metal beads, and ceramic beads. I'm going to highlight some of the beads used in my designs.

Ceramic beads come in several shapes and may be glazed or similarly textured.

Crystal beads have multiple machine-cut facets that capture the light and reflect it with lots of sparkle. They come in dozens of colors, sizes, and shapes.

Faux pearls have a synthetic coating over a crystal, glass, or plastic base. They are very uniform in size, shape, and color. Freshwater pearls are not uniform in size and shape, but have a very natural look.

Faux Pearls

Glass beads come in all sizes, shapes, and colors. Some have an AB (aurora borealis) finish, while others are polished to a high luster. There are also matte finish glass beads available.

Crystal Beads

Metal beads, including bead caps and spacers, can be made of base metal or plated metals.

Metal Beads

Glass Beads

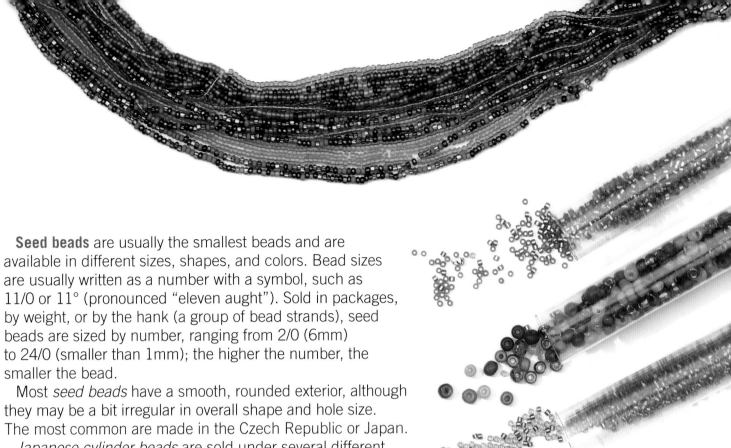

Seed beads are usually the smallest beads and are available in different sizes, shapes, and colors. Bead sizes are usually written as a number with a symbol, such as 11/0 or 11° (pronounced "eleven aught"). Sold in packages, by weight, or by the hank (a group of bead strands), seed beads are sized by number, ranging from 2/0 (6mm) to 24/0 (smaller than 1mm); the higher the number, the smaller the bead.

Most *seed beads* have a smooth, rounded exterior, although they may be a bit irregular in overall shape and hole size. The most common are made in the Czech Republic or Japan.

Japanese cylinder beads are sold under several different brand names—Delicas, Treasures, and Aikos. Very consistent in size and shape, these little tube beads have very large round holes and straight sides and are perfect for creating a flat, even-textured piece of beadwork.

Other types of seed beads include *bugle beads*, which are long, thin tubular beads and come in 2mm to 30mm lengths.

Shell beads have a lustrous finish. They can be uniform in size, shape, and color or be more varied and organic.

Seed Beads

Shell Beads

Bugle Beads

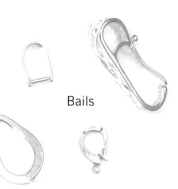

WildFire™
Beading Thread

Nylon-coated
Stringing Wire

FINDINGS

Findings are the components used to assemble jewelry.

Bails are attached to beads and other objects to create pendants. They come in many sizes, shapes, and designs. Some bails have prongs that fold over the bead and fit in the bead holes. Others have a loop with a flat "pad" attached, to which you can adhere an object. Some bails have hinges, making them easy to add to or remove from a necklace.

WildFire™ beading thread is a stringing material that is very strong and has very little stretch; it is a great choice for beadwork. The thread will not fray at the ends making it easy to thread through a needle and to tie knots.

Bails

Clasps

Chains

Nylon-coated stringing wire is made up of multiple strands of metal that are twisted together and coated with nylon; the more strands, the stronger and more flexible the wire. The nylon coating protects the wires from the abrasive areas of some beads.

Chains come in a variety of sizes, styles, colors, and finishes.

Clasps of all sizes, shapes, and styles abound. *Lobster clasps* are shaped like a lobster's claw and have a spring-action closure. *Slide clasps* consist of a bar and a tube that slide together and are held in place with a magnet or a spring friction mechanism. The bar and tube have loops to accommodate multiple strands. A *toggle clasp* is secured by sliding the bar through the ring. *Magnetic clasps* hold the necklace or bracelet closed with a magnet in each half of the clasp.

Leather Cord

Leather Lace

Cord ends fit over the ends of leather, rubber, satin, or other types of cord. Some are meant to be crimped in place with flat-nose or chain-nose pliers. Others are held in place with jeweler's glue.

Crimp beads and tubes are small metal beads and tubes that are flattened over the stringing wire to finish the ends or hold elements in place. The beads are rounded and the tubes are cylinder-shaped. Both come in many sizes and finishes.

Head pins and eye pins are very similar and are used in similar situations when making jewelry. Head pins are a straight wire with a head of some sort; many are flat, but there are several decorative styles as well, such as a ball head. Eye pins are also a straight wire, but they have a loop at one end. This loop may be opened and closed with pliers, just like a jump ring (page 88).

Jump rings are metal rounds or ovals that are used to attach jewelry components to each other. The rings are opened and closed with 2 pairs of pliers (page 88).

Leather cord and lace come in a variety of sizes and colors and are used for a more casual look.

Solid rings, also known as soldered rings, are metal rings that are not cut like jump rings.

Cord Ends

Crimp Beads and Tubes

Head Pins and Eye Pins

Jump Rings

Leather Lace

TOOLS

These descriptions and photos will be useful when purchasing your jewelry-making tools.

The two most common types of **beading needle** are the flexible wire needle and the rigid metal needle. The eye of the flexible wire needle collapses on itself, making it easier to go through small hole beads.

Bead mats are made of foam-like material and keep the beads from rolling all over the work surface.

Bead boards are very handy when making jewelry. Not only can you see your necklace or bracelet in its final arrangement, the board also has measurements that are very helpful when laying out the design. Bead boards come in several sizes. Choose the board that fits your needs.

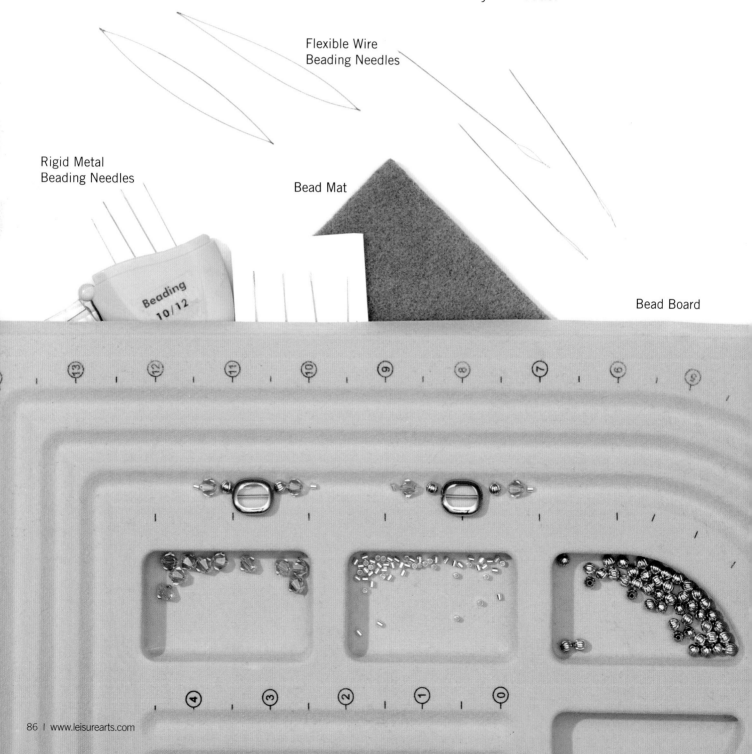

Flexible Wire
Beading Needles

Rigid Metal
Beading Needles

Bead Mat

Bead Board

Chain-nose Pliers

Chain-nose pliers have rounded, tapered jaws and a flat interior surface that will not mar wire. These pliers are used for reaching into tight places, gripping objects, opening and closing jump rings, and bending wire. They may also be called needle-nose pliers.

Flat-nose pliers have flat, tapered jaws and a flat interior surface. These pliers are used to hold wire, beads, and other components without scratching. The flat interior surface is great for making sharp bends and angles in wire, flattening wire or metal, and opening and closing jump rings.

Flat-nose Pliers

Round-nose pliers have round jaws that are useful for making loops and bending wire smoothly.

Wire cutters are used to cut small gauge wire, beading wire, head pins, eye pins, and other soft wires.

Crimping pliers (also known as a crimping tool) flatten and shape the crimp bead or crimp tube and are available in different sizes to work with the crimp bead and crimp tube sizes available.

Round-nose Pliers

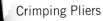
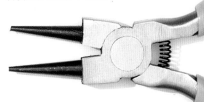

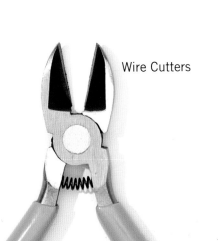
Wire Cutters

Crimping Pliers

Basic Terms & Techniques

Pick up Beads

Slide new beads onto the beading needle or wire.

Pass the Needle Through

Pass the beading needle, threaded with the working beading thread, through the indicated beads. Pass the needle back through means that the needle will pass through beads that have been passed through before.

Opening and Closing Jump Rings

Whether you need to attach a clasp, a charm or dangle, or other jewelry component, you'll probably use jump rings. Here's how to properly open and close them.

Pick up a jump ring with flat-nose pliers. With chain-nose pliers, gently hold the other side of the ring. Open the ring by pulling one pair of pliers toward you while pushing the other away *(Photo 1)*.

Close the ring by pushing and pulling the pliers in the opposite direction, bringing the ring ends back together. Once both ends are together, tweak 3-4 times back and forth, as if you can't decide to leave it open or closed and then finally close the ring. Tweaking helps to harden the wire and makes the ring more secure.

Making Loops on Head Pins and Eye Pins

Slide your beads onto a head pin or eye pin. Leaving about $1/2$" of wire at the end, cut off the excess wire. If you are making a large loop, leave more wire at the end.

Using chain-nose pliers, bend the wire at a 90° angle *(Photo 2)*. Holding the pin with chain-nose pliers, grasp the very tip of the wire with the round-nose pliers. Turn the pliers and bend the wire into a loop *(Photo 3)*. Release the pliers. Straighten or twist the loop further if necessary.

Photo 1

Photo 2

Photo 3

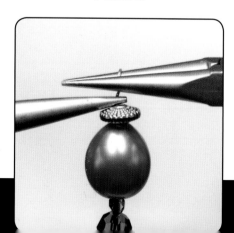

Adding Crimp Beads and Tubes

To finish a wire end or hold a bead or other element in place, string a crimp bead or tube on the wire. Place the bead or tube on the inner groove of the crimping pliers and squeeze *(Photo 4)*.

Release the pliers, turn the bead or tube a quarter turn, and place it in the outer groove. Squeeze the pliers to round out the crimping bead or tube *(Photo 5)*.

Finishing Leather Cord Ends With Crimp Tubes with Loops

Simply slide one crimp tube onto the leather cord end. Make sure the cord end is completely inside the tube. Using chain-nose pliers, press the tube area firmly, being careful not to break it.

To add a clasp, open the jump ring on the clasp and slide on one of the crimp tube loops; close the ring. The opposite crimp tube loop can serve as the ring to hook the clasp or you can add a jump ring for a larger loop.

Finishing Wire Ends With Solid Rings

Slide a crimp bead or crimp tube and a solid ring on the stringing wire. Pass the wire back through the crimp bead or tube, so that the wire loops through the ring. Pull the wire taut, but not so tight as to inhibit movement *(Photo 6)*. Using the crimping pliers, close the crimp bead or tube. Trim off the excess wire.

Tying a Half Hitch Knot

Pass the needle under a thread between 2 beads in the beadwork. Pass the needle through the loop and tighten *(Fig. 1)*, pulling the knot into the beadwork. Repeat several times to secure the thread. Half-hitch knots may also be tied with the beginning tail and the working thread.

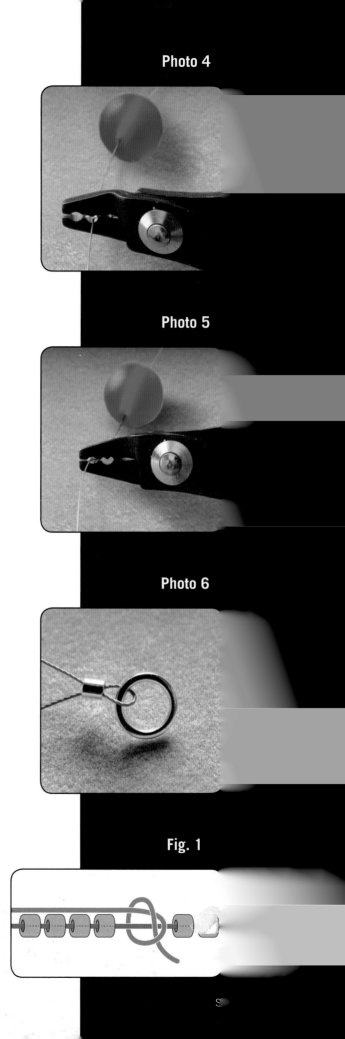

Photo 4

Photo 5

Photo 6

Fig. 1

BEADWORK TECHNIQUES

Starting the Beadwork

Many of the project instructions will tell you to begin with a "**comfortable length of thread**." This will vary for each person, but try this: raise your arm above your head, holding a threaded needle. Double the thread and cut at the shoulder level. Slide the needle so you are only using a single thread for beadwork. As you work, you'll figure out what length suits you.

Tip: Too long a thread length and you will really work for each stitch; too short a thread length and you will end and start new threads very often.

An **anchor bead** is temporary and keeps the project beads on the thread. Choose a bead that is a different color and size than the project beads; a size 6/0 or 8/0 seed bead usually works well. String this bead on the thread. Leaving a 6"-8" tail at the end of the thread, pass the needle through the bead twice. This creates 2 loops around the bead and keeps it from sliding. To remove the anchor bead, use a needle to loosen the loops and slide the bead off.

Securing the Thread in the Middle of the Beadwork

There are several ways to secure the thread. This is the method that I like the best. It's almost always better to hide the half hitch knots in the middle of your beadwork rather than on the edges.

1. Beginning between 2 beads and using your needle (still threaded with the working thread), tie 3 half hitch knots around a thread(s).

2. Pass through the 2-3 nearest beads and repeat the knotting process. Do this a few times, changing direction so the ending thread is not in a single straight line. Trim the excess thread after you've started a new thread.

Tip: Move in horizontal or vertical lines to keep the thread hidden inside the beadwork. When you change direction, make a turn around and pass the needle through the next bead in the reverse direction.

Starting A New Thread in the Middle of the Beadwork

Leaving a 6" tail, pass the needle through 2 beads a few rows away from the ending point of the previous thread. Pass the needle through the beads in the beadwork, tying half hitch knots between the beads. Pass the needle through the beads to get to the point where you left off. Continue the beadwork.

Ending the Thread

If the anchor bead is still attached, pass the needle (still threaded with the working thread) back and forth through the beadwork until you reach the anchor bead. Remove the anchor bead and tie 3 half hitch knots with the tail and working threads. Pass the working thread through the beadwork away from the tail and trim the excess. Pass the tail through the beadwork in the opposite direction and trim the excess.

If the anchor bead has been removed and the tail tied off, pass the needle through the 2-3 nearest beads and tie 3 half hitch knots. Do this a few times, changing direction so the thread is not in a straight line. Trim the excess thread.

PEYOTE STITCH

Pick up an even number of beads as indicated in the project. These shift as you work and become the first and second row of beads. Pick up another bead, skip the last bead previously strung on your thread and pass the needle through the next bead *(Fig. 2)*.

As you tighten the thread, notice that the new bead sits on top of the bead you skipped. Continue in this manner, picking up a bead, skipping a bead, and passing the needle through the next bead until you get to the end of the row *(Fig. 3)*. Notice that each new bead sits on top of the previous row's skipped bead. This shows the "up, down, offset by $\frac{1}{2}$ a bead" look of Peyote Stitch rows.

For the next row, pick up a bead, skip the low bead, and pass the needle through the top bead all the way across the row *(Fig. 4)*. Continue in this manner until you've worked the specified number of rows.

Fig. 2

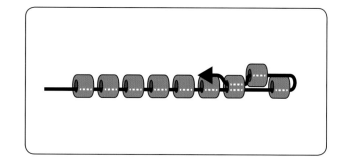

Fig. 3

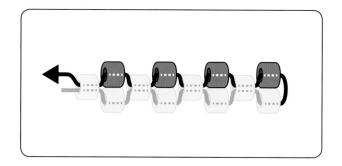

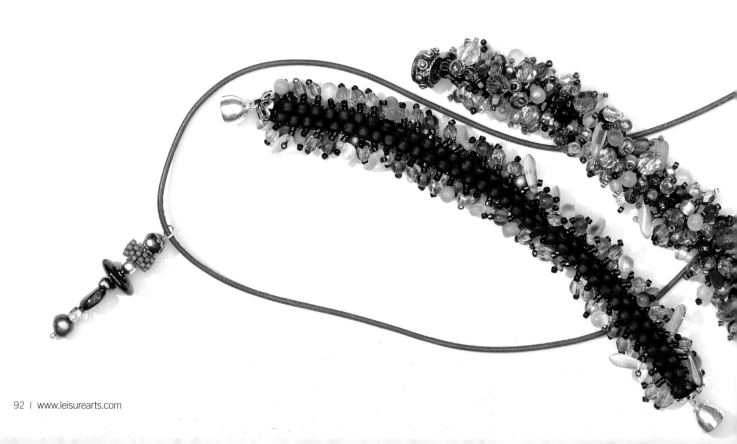

Counting Peyote Stitch Rows

Count the beads on each side of the beadwork. Add the two numbers together and that is the number of rows you have. The number of beads on each side should be the same to add up to the number of rows that the project specifies. For example, the project says to work 16 rows of Peyote Stitch. If the row count on one side is 7 and the row count on the other side is 8, work one more row of Peyote Stitch. If one row count is 9 and the other row count is 8, remove a row of beads to bring both sides to the same number.

Tip: *When ending a thread or adding a new thread, keep the threads hidden by moving in a zigzag pattern* **(Fig. 5)**.

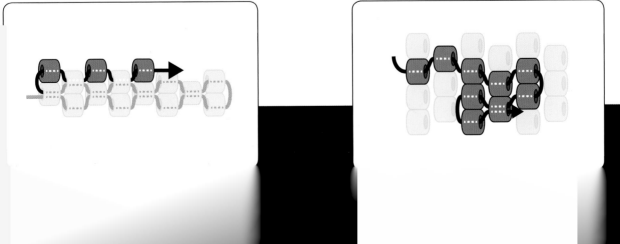

Fig. 4   **Fig. 5**

SQUARE STITCH

Pick up the number of beads as indicated in the project. Pick up another bead and pass the needle back through the last bead on the previous row. Pass the needle back through the bead you just added. Repeat to add the next bead *(Fig. 6)*.

Some projects require you to pick up 2 or 3 beads at a time; in that case, simply double or triple the number of beads that you pass the needle back through on the previous row. For example, if you pick up 2 beads, pass the needle back through 2 beads on the previous row.

Continue in this manner to work the number of rows as indicated in the project instructions. After the last row, pass the needle back through all the rows in the reverse direction to reinforce the beadwork *(Fig. 7)*.

Counting Square Stitch Rows
In Square Stitch, you only count the rows on one side of your beadwork to determine the number of rows completed.

Tip: When ending a thread or adding a new thread, keep the threads hidden by moving in straight lines, reversing direction every so often *(Fig. 8)*.

Fig. 6

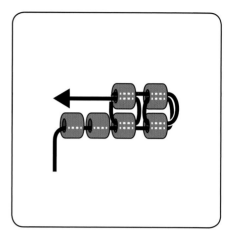

Fig. 7

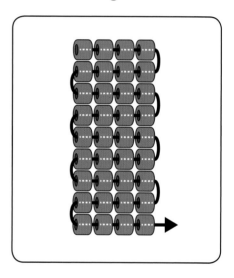

Fig. 8

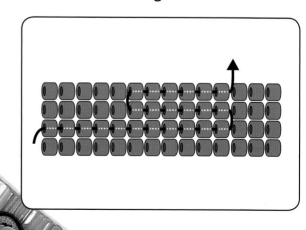

BEADWORK GRIDS

These grids will come in handy if you'd like to design a pendant in either Peyote Stitch or Square Stitch. Color the design in with colored pencils and use it as your bead weaving chart.

Square Stitch

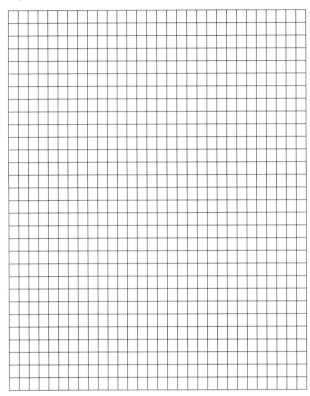

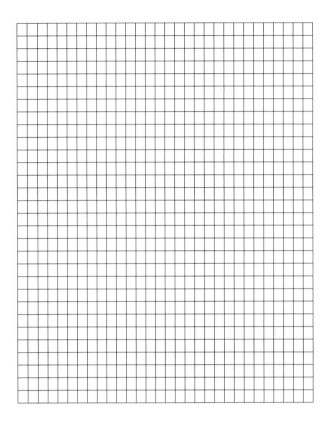

Peyote Stitch

SOURCES

Thanks to these suppliers and manufacturers, who contributed many of the products I used for these designs.

Aleene's® Jewelry and Metal Glue™ by iLoveToCreate
www.iLoveToCreate.com

Amazing Casting Resin and Mold Putty by Alumilite Corp.
www.AmazingMoldPutty.com

Bead Knots
www.BeadKnots.com

Beadalon®
www.Beadalon.com

Blue Moon Beads® by Creativity Inc.
www.CreativityInc.com

Diamond Tech Fuseworks by Diamond Tech
www.DiamondTechGlass.com

E-6000® adhesive by Eclectic Products, Inc.
www.EclecticProducts.com

Excel Hobby Blades Corp.
www.ExcelHobbyBlades.com

Jacquard Products
www.JacquardProducts.com

Jolee's Jewels by EK Success Brands
www.EKSuccessBrands.com

Realeather® Jewelry by Silver Creek Leather Company
www.SilverCreekLeather.com

Royal® & Langnickel Brush Mfg.
www.RoyalBrush.com

31901050962861